UNSPOKEN WORDS

A Descendant of Stillwater Pioneers Discovers Her Ancestors

THERESA LYNNE MCGOLDRICK

Medley Books

Edited by Lauren Humphries-Brooks

Cover and interior design by Asya Blue

Index created by Sue Klefstad

Photo restorations by Meghan McGoldrick

Family trees and artwork created by Meghan McGoldrick

Proof editors Dianne Shutt and Michelle Fulmer

Publication Management by Eva Long; longonbooks.com

ISBN 978-1-7334147-0-8 (paperback)

ISBN 978-1-7334147-2-2 (hardcover)

ISBN 978-1-7334147-1-5 (ebook)

Library of Congress Control Number: 2019914020

Publisher's Cataloging-In-Publication Data

(Prepared by The Donohue Group, Inc.)

Names: McGoldrick, Theresa Lynne, author.

Title: Unspoken words : a descendant of Stillwater pioneers discovers her ancestors / Theresa Lynne McGoldrick.

Description: Apollo Beach, Florida : Medley Books, [2019] | Includes bibliographical references and index.

Identifiers: ISBN 9781733414708 (paperback) | ISBN 9781733414722 (hardcover) | ISBN 9781733414715 (ebook)

Subjects: LCSH: McGoldrick, Theresa Lynne--Family. | Wright family. | McLaggan family. | Stillwater (Minn.)--Genealogy. | Frontier and pioneer life--Minnesota--Stillwater--History. | Alden, John, 1599-1687--Family. | Mayflower (Ship) | LCGFT: Family histories. | Creative nonfiction.

Classification: LCC F614.S86 M34 2019 (print) | LCC F614.S86 (ebook) | DDC 929.20977659--dc23

Cover Image: Addison Wright (1841-1919). circa 1870

Courtesy of Jon Meister

Printed in the United States of America

First Edition

*Dedicated to my mother, Mary,
for her inspiration and love of our Stillwater family history.*

*Also dedicated to my daughter, Meghan,
for her assortment of inspirations and never-ending
encouragement.*

"Fill your paper with the breathings of your heart."
-William Wordsworth

Contents

Chapter Thirteen

Chapter Fourteen

Chapter Fifteen

Chapter Sixteen

PREFACE

I began my genealogy research efforts after my dad died in 2006. It became my private therapy as I continued with what seemed like a never-ending mourning process of a daughter losing her father. I loved seeing his name appear in documents and connecting those written sources with stories I heard over the years. I was captivated seeing the connections, learning stories about his family, and meeting extended family that I never knew I had.

Upon seeing my success at finding information on my dad's side of the family, my mother asked me if I would do some ancestral research for her, on her maternal side from Stillwater, Minnesota, fondly known to my family and me as "pioneers." My ancestors from Stillwater are the family my sisters and I heard the most about over the years, so I didn't think I would find anything new or out of the ordinary; however, my mother requested I do so. Maybe this type of time travel through her Stillwater memories would be good therapy for her after losing her partner and husband of over fifty-seven years. As I began the research on my maternal side of the family, the family I thought I knew the most about, little did I know what I would discover.

INTRODUCTION

As adults, many of us wish we had spent more time asking our parents and grandparents questions about their past. We'll get a few stories here and there when engaging in small conversations. As the years go by and we realize the past's importance, we're left without the luxury of communicating with our family on this subject, for various reasons. Because we realize this sometimes a bit too late, it becomes the duty of the descendants to work through the clues left behind by our ancestors.

Nothing resonated with me more about the lives of my ancestors than the unspoken words I found in various written sources and periodicals throughout my research. As I sifted through vital records, church records, obituaries, newspaper articles, and other sources, I began to meet my ancestors.

This ancestry and storybook I present to you is a small contribution about the lives of three separate families who arrived during the early development of the lumber and logging town of Stillwater, considered the Birthplace of Minnesota.

These three families, who migrated from areas such as Ireland, Canada, Maine, and New York, were unknown to each other at the time of their arrivals in Stillwater. However, the Tobins, the Wrights, and the McLaggans would become connected by future generations through the lives of their descendants. The legacy of these pioneer families continues to this day, as many of their descendants still occupy homes and live their daily lives in Stillwater, other towns in Washington County, various regions of Minnesota, and throughout the United States.

These pioneer families were not necessarily the "movers and shakers" of the historic lumber town like the men from Maine, such as Elam Greeley and John McKusick, two of Stillwater's original founders,[1] or lumber baron Isaac

Staples, who owned a mansion where Pioneer Park is today, overlooking his sawmill and the famous river town.[2] There were also other early and prominent settlers who contributed to Stillwater's history, whose names line the streets, reminding current-day residents of the legacies they left behind.

Many immigrants who came to Stillwater as pioneers from different parts of our country and the world also contributed to building the town we know and love today. Some of the immigrants who lived and worked alongside some of its founders are all but forgotten.

These "ordinary" people housed lumbermen and laborers while raising a family. They worked, lived, and worshipped right alongside the more famous founders and residents of Stillwater. They had some triumphs and endured tragedy, sometimes without even a statement announcing their end in the local newspaper.

I feel fortunate that I have been able to discover some of my family's history and to have obtained a pocket-sized peek into their past. I can't report on all of their everyday activities in Stillwater; however, I can speculate on a portion of their lives, using vital records, publications, and other sources, as well as some stories that family members had spoken of throughout the years. Even though it's a small portion of their lives that I'm sharing with you, this research allowed me to know and appreciate where my family came from. I discovered the struggles they endured and events they celebrated while trying to create prosperous lives for themselves, their families, and future generations.

Along with discoveries based on my research, this book also contains stories from family members, as well as some of my own writings concerning what I imagine happened at different times during an ancestor's life. Many times I had to begin with stories and assumptions which then led to research to find the documents. It was through my research and finding the evidence in written documents when the stories that were relayed to me over the years were validated and a sigh of relief and feeling of accomplishment would follow. However, there were times my assumptions had to end just at that, and an ancestor's life had to remain only in my thoughts and what I imagined became of their lives.

You will also find other names sprinkled throughout the book, which may or may not be related to these three families; however, they were associated with my Stillwater ancestors in some way or another throughout the years since the beginning of their arrival in the mid-1850s.

This book of research and writings is intended to share ancestral history with my family, immediate and extended, and anyone else who may be interested in ancestry, genealogical research, or a bit of Stillwater history.

I try to be as accurate as possible with the information I have put forth; however, some past records caused me to question their validity from time to time. That's when I used my genealogist experience and training to connect unrelated information to come to a reasonable conclusion.

During my research, I also found misspelled words contained in several of the newspaper articles. I included the original misspellings in the articles within the book, to continue the fabric of the era.

I also want to give insight into the different kinds of research and sources I used to assist me in reaching my conclusions about my relatives, demonstrating how the unspoken words in written sources can help others when writing their own creative family histories. These sources will be found within the pages of this book, as well as being listed in the sources and bibliography sections.

I was born and raised in St. Paul, Stillwater's sister-city of days gone by; however, Stillwater has always played a large part of my and my family's life, as far back as I can remember.

This book is my way of remembering my family's legacy, when my ancestors entered as pioneers to Stillwater, the Birthplace of Minnesota.

PART ONE

CHAPTER ONE

My Mother's Request

The Story Was the Wright Brothers

When I was young, my mother spoke very highly and very often of her family from Stillwater, Minnesota. She was always told by her grandmother, Ivy, known to her grandchildren as Nana, that they were related to the Wright Brothers. Her grandmother's maiden name was Wright, and so naturally, Nana always relayed that bit of exciting piece of information to her eleven grandchildren quite regularly. This is the story my sisters and I, and our cousins, first and second, heard all the time. Of course we believed it—why wouldn't we? It was an exceptional story to share with our closest friends. Many years passed since I first heard this celebrated claim, and I decided it was time to begin my mother's research request and find out just how we were related to the dynamic flying duo.

My mother reminded me of a few names of our Stillwater ancestors that were written on a somewhat aged piece of paper, tucked safely away in her family Bible. She first gave me the name of her grandmother, Ivy (Wright) McLaggan, who was adored by all her grandchildren. She then gave me the names of Ivy Wright's parents, Addison Wright and Anna Maria Tobin, and Ivy Wright's husband's name, John McLaggan. That was enough for me to get started.

I began my research scouring everything I could find on the most popular ancestry websites, looking for Orville and Wilbur's names to pop up or give me a hint regarding our family relationship ties. Alas, nothing showed for my family being related to the trail-blazing pilots. Feeling disappointed and moderately defeated, I continued my investigation on every ancestry tree that resembled mine, and two names continued to appear, with a reference to the Mayflower: John Alden and Priscilla Mullins.

The Story Becomes the *Mayflower*

I was feeling somewhat reluctant to tell my mother about not being successful in trying to trace our family to the Wright Brothers. As a few days passed, I knew it was time to give her a call. When I phoned her and relayed this information to her, I could sense it wasn't well received, as there was a somewhat lengthy silence on the other end of the phone. However, when I told her about my findings of John Alden and Priscilla Mullins, the conversation began again. She began to quote a line from a poem written by Henry Wadsworth Longfellow, which she learned in grade school about the Pilgrim couple: "Why don't you speak for yourself, John," she proclaimed. I knew she would be pleased to hear this information, as I remember her quoting that same line from the poem on many Thanksgiving Days of the past.

My mother seemed so excited to learn that she might be related to John and Priscilla that the Wright Brothers became an afterthought.

I set the Wright Brothers mystery aside for the time being, and continued to look into the interesting love story of the *Mayflower* passengers, John and Priscilla, who not only survived the journey on the *Mayflower*, but also the first winter that so many of the 102 passengers did not, including Priscilla's parents and her younger brother. Priscilla was only 17 when her family perished that first winter, leaving her orphaned in the new world in Plymouth.[3]

I located Longfellow's endearing story, classified as a poem mentioned by my mother, and read it in its entirety for the first time: *The Courtship of Miles Standish*.[4] The poem is Longfellow's thoughts on what may have occurred between three *Mayflower* passengers; Miles Standish, John Alden, and Priscilla Mullins. Captain Standish's wife also died during the first winter after arriving at Plymouth, and both he and John Alden admired the young and recently orphaned Priscilla Mullins. The captain, being the superior to the younger John Alden, as well as his friend, asked John to approach Priscilla to ask her if she would accept Standish's proposal of marriage. This, of course, was very difficult for John, as he longed for Priscilla's hand in marriage as well. It seems there was a minor love triangle going on in the early 1620s. When John presented Priscilla with the captain's marriage proposal, she was also taken aback, as she herself had her designs on John Alden. According to Longfellow's poem, the last sentence in Part III, her reply was, "Why don't you speak for yourself, John."[5] We know how the story ends, and John and Priscilla get married; however, Captain Standish wasn't very happy about the outcome. I don't want to give away any of the other details, as you may find you may want to read Longfellow's poem for yourself. Longfellow writes a good story; a bit long. Historical? Possibly. Perhaps historical fiction.

My mother was very appreciative and excited to learn about her *Mayflower* ancestry, although I know she still wonders if there is a Wright Brothers connection. During research in the future, I would love nothing more than to be able to find a connection to the Wright Brothers and for this beloved story that has been spoken of throughout several generations to be true. Perhaps someday I will knock down a genealogy brick wall and our connection to them will appear. Even to this day, the five remaining grandchildren of Ivy (Wright) McLaggan repeat this claim with unwavering conviction, just because Ivy (Wright) McLaggan, the Nana they all adored and thought the world of, said it was so.

After finding the connection to the *Mayflower* through my research, I decided to look into becoming a member of the General Society of *Mayflower* Descendants, headquartered in Plymouth.[6] For myself to become an approved member of the Society, I had to provide them with vital records, and other documentation to prove an unbroken family lineage of many generations to create my ancestral pedigree, which would connect myself to my ancestor, John Alden.

The records that were required from me to obtain and subsequently submit to the society were: birth records, death records, church records, wills, probate records, obituaries, cemetery records, or anything else that would confirm a connection with each and every one of my direct-line of ancestors, also known as grandparents from many generations, continuing through to myself.

When unable to locate a vital record, one of the most important and valuable documents I found during my research was that of an ancestor's obituary, written lovingly by the families of the past. Many people correlate an obituary with death; however, I like to correlate an obituary with life. These mini biographies, published in local newspapers and read by many distant relatives and citizens of years gone by, was one of the ways I was able to meet and get to know my ancestors. As I read these beautiful life stories over and over again, I contemplated who these individuals were, where they came from, and the impact they made on the lives of others.

After a few years of on-again/off-again research and visits to Stillwater cemeteries, historical societies, libraries, and the like, I submitted eight generations of ancestry research to the General Society of *Mayflower* Descendants in Plymouth, Massachusetts. The historians and genealogists at the General Society carefully examined and scrutinized each document and source I submitted in great detail for accuracy. I was elated the day I received the approval and validation of my documentation from the General Society of *Mayflower* Descendants, proving that I am a direct descendant of John Alden and Priscilla (Mullins) Alden through my family, the Wrights, who located to Stillwater, Minnesota in the 1860s.

A thought that crossed my mind after receiving my approval was how ironic it was to learn that Henry Wadsworth Longfellow, the author of the poem my mother quoted that started me on my quest regarding John and Priscilla of the *Mayflower*, was a distant cousin of mine, as he is also a direct descendant of John and Priscilla Alden.

Researching my Wright Family and connected ancestors who migrated to Stillwater, and having to provide their documentation to the *Mayflower* Society, forced me to get to know them in a way I never knew possible. I became so aware of their personalities that I felt like I had truly met them. Learning of their stories in a more complete way, and reading through their official documents and vital records, helped me to know who they were, where they came from, and how they lived their lives. I felt like I was meeting them for the first time, and began to feel a familial and emotional connection to them. I celebrated their births, enjoyed their stories and photographs, and mourned their deaths as if it was a beloved family member I had already known. Now that I had completed the journey of researching and validating my ancestral connection to John and Priscilla Alden of the *Mayflower*, how could I just set aside these documents of this newly discovered legacy?

I read once that the spirits of our loved ones who have gone before us are kept alive when we continually speak of them. These newly found sources, particularly obituaries, at many times spoke for themselves.

It didn't seem right for me to ignore these interesting life stories when these distant family members of mine had become such a big part of my life. I decided I wanted to relay their stories to their descendants, as I believe the best thing we can do for our ancestors and family members who have passed on is to remember them by keeping their stories alive, for years to come.

Remember Your Beginnings

"*R*emember who you are and remember where you came from." This is a phrase my sisters and I, and our cousins, would hear quite often from our parents while we were growing up. A phrase our parents heard from their mother from Stillwater. A phrase that should be easy to understand. But I'm not quite sure what it refers to, exactly, although it seems obvious.

Were they talking about coming from Stillwater, or coming from a good family? Or perhaps it was a phrase handed down from family members many years ago, who knew we were descendants of John and Priscilla Alden of the *Mayflower,* and that part of family history got lost in translation over the years? Maybe it was just a simple saying that meant, "Watch your P's and Q's," which basically means mind your manners—especially when you're out and about because you're representing the family. Perhaps it's a saying that was handed down through generations referring to exactly what it means: "remember where you're from." Whatever its origins or the exact meaning, it's a phrase that our family repeats to each other when we get together, in a somewhat humorous way at times, that accompanies a very special feeling and endearing message whenever it is spoken.

CHAPTER TWO

Approaching Stillwater

They Were Pioneers

"We're here! There's the St. Croix River." I could see in my mother's eyes the absolute love she had for the little town of her past and present relatives that she always spoke of to my sisters and me as we entered Main Street.

While I was growing up on the East Side of St. Paul in the 1960s and 1970s, my family and I would often travel the approximately twenty-five-minute trip to Stillwater, Minnesota, which seemed much longer, to visit my mother's aunt Jean and her family for picnics at Pioneer Park, or historical walks or drives through town.

To get to Stillwater from our home in St. Paul, my father drove east on Highway 36. When we were getting closer to Stillwater, he veered left onto Highway 95 and began to travel parallel to the river. Within minutes, Highway 95 was transformed into Main Street, Stillwater. I will always remember the delight that would come across my mother's face as Minnesota's majestic St. Croix River was finally in sight. Directly across the St. Croix River was the state of Wisconsin. As a young girl, knowing that I could see another state at the same time as being in Minnesota gave me a somewhat "worldly" feeling of excitement and adventure.

I often wonder if all of my mother's experiences, or the stories about her family that were relayed to her over the years, were passing in front of her eyes as we passed by all the "frozen-in-time" shops, family establishments, and, two streets over, St. Michael's Catholic Church at Third and Walnut

Streets, where her mother and prior generations had been parishioners.

As my five sisters and I began to feel as if we were traveling back in time when we drove onto Main Street, one of the first things our mother would always remind us of was what her grandmother, Ivy (Wright) McLaggan, told her about her family. "They were pioneers!" I heard it all the time from my mother. Because of hearing it often, I usually didn't pay too much attention to the constant reminder of our "pioneer legacy." Unfortunately, I really didn't care about family history at all at that time. Learning of people whom I didn't know anything about or feel I had a connection with wasn't a big interest to me. As we arrived in Stillwater, I was more interested with the sights and sounds I experienced, as if entering a world lost in time. I couldn't wait to get out of the car and walk up the steep steps, beginning on Main Street, to view the town from above. I was enchanted with window shopping, where my ancestors did likewise over a century ago–that didn't sink in either.

Little did I know at the time that many years after our weekend adventures to Stillwater, I would be spending hours upon hours researching my family's beginnings in the Birthplace of Minnesota.

CHAPTER THREE
The Tobin Family

The Tobin Family

John Tobin m. Margaret Cunningham**

1810-1889   1828 - Unknown

Their Children

Richard

1849 - 1913

Anna Maria*

1850 - 1875

Margaret

1855 - Unknown

John, Jr

1858 - 1913

Catherine

1859 - 1892

James

1861 - Unknown

*Direct Ancestors

*"**Anna Maria was born in Maine and a young pioneer when she came to Stillwater.**"* — Mary Brown-Kirst

The clearest memories I have about learning who my great-great-grandmother Anna Maria Tobin was is that she was born in Maine and a young pioneer when she arrived in Stillwater. These two verbal facts, always combined within the same sentence, were consistently relayed to me by my mother regarding family history and our pioneer beginnings.

The Pioneers Begin Their Journey

When Anna Maria's father, Irish immigrant John Tobin, began his journey from Ireland to America, did he realize there would be some hardships that would appear in his future from time to time? Before his journey from Ireland began, I'm sure he didn't expect just how difficult those hardships and personal losses would be.

John Tobin migrated to America from Ireland sometime before 1848. After he arrived on the shores of America, he settled in Bangor, Maine. At the time of his arrival, Bangor was considered the lumber capital of the world, and one of the busiest ports that served the East Coast.[7]

After he settled in Maine, he met and married Margaret Cunningham, also of Irish descent, although said to have been from New Brunswick, Canada. The two married in Bangor in 1848.[8]

Margaret's younger sister of two years, Mary Ann Cunningham, married Irish immigrant John Felix O'Brien, also in Bangor, one year later, in 1849.[9]

While living in Maine, Margaret and John Tobin began their family, and Margaret gave birth to two children. The oldest, Richard, was born in 1849, and their second child, Anna Maria, was born in 1850.

Margaret's younger sister, Mary Ann, and her husband, John Felix O'Brien, also began their family in Maine before migrating to Stillwater.

With their small children in tow, the Tobins and O'Briens started their journey west to Stillwater, arriving sometime before 1856, when Minnesota was still considered a territory.

Even though there were a few other towns becoming populated at the same time, it was Stillwater that hosted the territorial convention in 1848 that began the process of Minnesota becoming an official state. The approving results of the convention proclaimed Minnesota as a territory in 1849. It was because of the territorial convention held in Stillwater that the up-and-coming logging and lumber town became known as "the Birthplace of Minnesota."[10] Nine years later, on May 11, 1858, the admittance of Minnesota as the thirty-second state in the Union was passed by Congress and approved by President James Buchanan.[11]

As Bangor was said to be the lumber capital of the world during the time of the Tobins' and O'Briens' arrival in America, why did the young families leave it for a similar logging town of Stillwater, approximately 1400 miles northwest?

The lumber industry was growing quickly in Stillwater, with its added population mostly from Maine.[12] Some even predicted it would become the next Bangor,[13] which may have been a deciding factor for the Tobins' and O'Briens' departure and subsequent journey to Stillwater.

The Tobins' Boarding House

Due to the growing population in Stillwater at the time of the Tobins' arrival, the small family began to take in out-of-town laborers, and thus their home became a boarding house. Their home was located somewhere within the original town of Stillwater, considered as the North Hill area, which was platted in 1848.[14]

Margaret Tobin was still giving birth to her and John's children in the late 1850s, when the family first opened their doors to the out-of-town guests. They shared their home with strangers, mostly men, while raising their young family. The couple went on to have several more children within the first few years of their arrival to Stillwater.

Their first child born in Stillwater, although third in line of the Tobin children, was another daughter born in 1856 whom they named Margaret Ellen. During that time, not only was the size of the Tobin family beginning to increase, the population of Stillwater was as well.

IN THE NEWS

The Stillwater Messenger, October 6, 1857

The Growth of Stillwater.

From the Stillwater Messenger of August 4th, we learn that the present population of Stillwater is full four-thousand, being an increase of 3,100 in two and a quarter years, of 344 per-cent.

In 1857, when the family shared their home with their boarders, the three Tobin children were the ages of nine, eight, and almost one. The several boarders living in the Tobin household and listed in the 1857 Minnesota Territorial Census were: Mary Cronan, from Ireland; Wm Ellet, from Maine; and John Durgan, George Burns, and Joseph Sutton, all listing their place of birth as New Brunswick.

John, Jr., was the next Tobin child to be born in Stillwater in 1858. One year later, another daughter, Catherine, was born, and given the lifelong nickname of "Cassie."

What was going through the minds of the young children while having to share their home with these ambitious and burly-looking fellows, never knowing what type of character would be entering over the threshold of their home on any given day? I'm sure these bedraggled, rugged men returned each evening after an exhausting and grueling day of their lumberjack trade, anxious to fill up on a good meal and go to bed. In the early morning, they would awake to a cup of black coffee and the town newspaper, then begin their strenuous day all over again.

It was because of the dedication of these hard-working men, well over a century ago, migrating from Ireland, Canada, Maine, or wherever else the growing logging town of Stillwater was calling out for lumberjacks and laborers, that assisted in the development and economy of Stillwater, and Minnesota.

IN THE NEWS

The Stillwater Messenger, September 22, 1857

THE NEW HOTEL—The new Hotel building of Messrs. Buck and Sawyer is progressing with commendable activity. It will be an ornament and a blessing to our city when completed. We have heretofore given its dimensions. It will be one of the largest in the territory.

THE LAKE HOUSE—This large building is now being raised to conform with the grade of Main street. We understand that another story is to be added, and the building otherwise thoroughly repaired, when it will be reopened as a Hotel, with new proprietors.

The Stillwater Messenger, September 29, 1857

Gas Light—The streets of St. Paul were lighted with gas last Saturday evening for the first time. Everything worked to a charm. That will do for an eight year old town, at the head of steamboat navigation on the Upper Mississippi.

The Stillwater Messenger, May 18, 1858

REJOICING—On the evening of the reception of the news of the admission of our State, a number of people gave expression of their gratification of the event by bonfires and a salute of thirty-two guns—the last one being for the State of Minnesota. May our State or the country never have cause to feel ashamed of the last born, or to regret the consummation of the important event.

The Stillwater Messenger, November 16, 1858

Lincoln for President.

An enthusiastic meeting at Mansfield, Ohio, a few days since, hoisted the name of Hon. ABRAHAM LINCOLN for the next presidency. The Galena Advertisers says: "We shall not be surprised to hear that this motion is seconded."

St. Michael's Catholic Church

The Tobins were Irish Catholics and belonged to St Michael's Catholic Church. St. Michael's was one of the earliest formed Catholic parishes in the state of Minnesota. Between the years 1849–1853, the early Catholic settlers of Stillwater, including the members of St. Michael's, were having their church services at the private homes of the parishioners. Visiting priests would travel from various areas to say Mass, traveling via a stagecoach route between the two cities, which included visits from Bishop Cretin of St. Paul.

As Stillwater and St. Michael's parish continued to grow, it became much harder to accommodate the parishioners at in-home masses. So the parishioners and Bishop Cretin decided to build a church in 1853, located in the North Hill area at Fourth and Mulberry Streets. The property was purchased from John McKusick.[15]

The baptism of the youngest Tobin daughter in 1859, Catherine Tobin, known as Cassie, was celebrated on the same day with her cousin, Martin O'Brien, son of her aunt Mary Ann (Cunningham) and uncle John Felix O'Brien. Church records indicate the two were baptized together on June 4, 1859. Martin O'Brien was only three days old at the time of his baptism, being born on June 1, 1859. Sadly, the O'Briens' young son, Martin, cousin to the Tobin children, didn't live to be even one year old.

A Grand Demonstration in Stillwater

In the *Stillwater Messenger*, dated July 12, 1859, a lengthy article entitled, "A Grand Demonstration in Stillwater," described the very successful event the city of Stillwater hosted to celebrate the anniversary of our National Independence on the Fourth of July, 1859. There was concern that the event wouldn't be well attended by the local community or citizens of nearby vicinities as there was rain in the morning continuing until noon. The officials of the city were surprised to see the throngs of citizens and strangers, numbered from five to eight thousand persons, lining the streets showing their enthusiastic patriotism before the rain had ended. When the rain subsided and the clouds dispersed, the sun was brightly shining, leaving a refreshing and pleasant atmosphere, and the townspeople were able to begin with their festivities.

The Armory building and homes around town were heavily decorated with patriotic buntings, banners and flags. When the parade participants assembled and were ready to begin, the Afton Brass Band was in the lead, followed by the Stillwater Guards and the Washington Light Artillery. The German Singing Society and other organizations also joined in the parade as it moved toward the destination where an official ceremony would take place. The parade included wagons and carriages pulled by horses and oxen, putting on a great display for the onlookers. One particular float was pulled by six horses carrying thirteen young ladies dressed all in white, representing the thirteen original states. Each young lady wore a badge bearing the name of the state she represented. The prominent float was covered with canvas and decorated with stars and stripes, banners, and evergreens.

Another float mentioned in the article stated it was of mammoth size, drawn by ten yoke of oxen, and furnished by the neighboring town of Oak Park. This float included seventy-six men, women, and children, who furnished forty baskets of food to share with all present during the Independence Day picnic. The huge endeavor and patriotic display put on by the residents of Oak Park received much applause. The men mentioned in the article who were responsible for such a large feat were Messrs. Nickerson, Forbes, Crofut, and Beach of Oak Park. Due to their generosity and patriotism, the citizens of Oak Park were granted free wharfage for a year.

When the procession reached Nelson's Grove, south of the city, the citizens drew their attention toward the river as they heard a loud firing of a cannon coming from the steamboat *Itasca*, announcing its arrival from St. Paul. Those disembarking the *Itasca*, anxious to join in the celebration, were the St. Paul Pioneer Guard and visiting excursionists from nearby towns, who would also partake in Stillwater's high-spirited Fourth of July celebration. Following their disembarkation, the St. Paul Military, the Pioneer Guard, and the governor's staff were greeted in military style and escorted to the speaker's stand. Stillwater and St. Paul officials alike offered several meaningful speeches and toasts. After the official ceremony and toasts at the stand were completed, the military companies assembled and demonstrated different intricate evolutions and manual of arms, which was enjoyed by the viewing spectators. When finished, they assembled and began their march back to the Armory.

However, the celebration was not quite finished, as there was an extravagant ball prepared for the social seekers of the city and their guests. The ball took place at the new Sawyer and Buck Hotel building beginning at 9 o'clock. The venue was described as being "festooned and decorated in the finest style."

The evening was full of good cheer, laughter, and dancing, until the dreaded whistle from the steamer *Itasca* reminded the St. Paul passengers of its midnight departure. Although the St. Paul guests unfortunately had to leave the event, the festivities continued throughout the night for the Stillwater residents, and the dancing and celebrating went on until a late hour in the morning. Overall, the city's patriotic celebration was a success. Even though there was a bit of rowdyism in the early part of the day, according to the paper, "the city was not disgraced either by violence or boisterous conduct."

IN THE NEWS

The Stillwater Messenger, December 20, 1859

SNOW STORM—A heavy snow storm set in on Saturday night last, and continued at intervals up to Monday morning. Only a few inches, however, of level snow have fallen, hardly sufficient to make sleighing. It is the earnest wish and hope of business men as well as pleasure seekers, that a suitable amount of snow for sleighing, may be vouchsafed to us before the holidays.

Back at the Boarding House

John Tobin's real estate value of his home and boarding house is stated as $500, in Stillwater's 1860 United States Federal Census record. At that time, the five Tobin children were the ages of eleven, ten, five, two, and one. This was the time the older children were instructed to help with the operation of the family's small enterprise. Richard, the oldest, helped in the kitchen, preparing meals as he anxiously awaited the return of the boarders each night, to hear the stories of the lumbermen's daily adventures out in the woods and upon the river. Their oldest daughter, Anna Maria, was in charge of her younger siblings, instructing them not to get in the way of their lumbermen guests, per Mother's orders. She may have also been assigned the task of picking up after these unknown laborers, as I'm sure a colossal mess followed them into the boarding house each night.

The names listed as living at the Tobins' boarding house in the 1860 Stillwater, Washington County Census, are described as "laborers," which could have been lumberjacks, carpenters, or any other profession needed as the town began to grow.

The names of the borders living with the family at that time were: Murdock Chisholm and George Burns, from New Brunswick; George Keys and William Jenkins from Maine; and Patrick Flannigan from Ireland. The last boarder's name listed in the 1860 Census is a bit hard to decipher. His first name is clearly written as James; however, his last name is a bit more challenging. It looks like it's written as Mulhavey, Mulaney, or possibly James Mulvey, who's recorded as an early settler to Stillwater in the 1850s. He first became a lumberman, then a businessman in several successful business endeavors within the lumber industry throughout the years.[16]

Deciphering census records can often be quite challenging, as whoever is trying to decode the names from the records of the past are at the mercy of the enumerator's handwriting.

When I reviewed the names, which were clearly written in past census records, I began to recognize the same names time and again during my research, and many of the last names I found continued in future records and publications over several generations. Recognizable names of the past are still present today in Stillwater, which makes the history and legacy of Stillwater much more tangible.

In 1860, one year after the spectacular Fourth of July celebration of 1859, there appeared in *The Stillwater Messenger* an article pertaining to where the citizens of Stillwater could travel to enjoy the 1860 Independence Day in neighboring towns. Apparently the city spent a bit too much money on the previous year's July Fourth celebration.

IN THE NEWS

The Stillwater Messenger, July 3, 1860

THE FOURTH—There will be no public celebration of the Fourth in this place. Our citizens observed the day last year on an extensive and ex-pensive scale, and this year many of them will leave town to participate in the festivities of the day with their neighbors.

The military and civic societies of St. Paul are making extensive preparations for an appropriate observance of the day. In our immediate neighborhood, we have heard of contemplated celebrations at Marine, Lakeland, Hudson, Prescott and Point Douglas. Our national bird will be active to-morrow.

The Stillwater Messenger, October 9, 1860

Cheap Traveling—During the past week passengers have been carried from St. Paul to Chicago for fifty cents, owing to competition between the various steamboat and Railroad lines. The fare has not exceeded one dollar for more than a fortnight past. Either the packet and railroad companies or our population will have to yield soon—they can't both hold out much longer. This has been the means of starting thousands on eastern journeys.

The Stillwater Messenger, December 18, 1860

CHRISTMAS—We are requested to announce that the ladies connected with the Universalist Society will erect a Christmas Tree at the Court house on Christmas Eve.

The Stillwater Messenger, March 26, 1861

The Lumber Business—The lumbermen continue to return from day to day from the pineries, though a large number of teams and men are yet actively engaged in getting out timber—the snow continuing good in the heavy timber. The past winter has been very favorable for this business. We have heard the amount of lumber that will be run out of the St. Croix the present season variously estimated at from 75,000,000 to 90,000,000 feet. Either figure might be compromised upon without detriment to our local interests. Fair prices is all that is needed to set our people on a whirl of prosperity.

More Tobin and O'Brien Baptisms

Catholic Church traditions and rules from the past are often different from today. Godparents may have been much younger in comparison with recent times. In 1861, eleven-year-old Anna Maria Tobin became the godmother to her infant cousin, James O'Brien, son of Mary Ann (Cunningham) and John Felix O'Brien, on March 17, 1861.

Margaret Tobin gave birth one more time in 1861 to a son. She and her husband named their newborn son, James, sharing the same name with his cousin. Two days after the Civil War erupted, he was baptized on April 14, 1861. Both infants were baptized by Father Thomas Murray.

IN THE NEWS

The Stillwater Messenger, January 7, 1862

Lieut. McGrety, of St. Paul has been in town for a few days enlisting men for St. Paul company for the fifth regiment. He took quite a number of men at Fort Snelling yesterday.

Changes Are Afoot for the Tobins

When the Tobins had been living in the place they called home for approximately seven years, increasing their family to six children, and keeping up with their daily lives of running a boarding house, the Tobin children were suddenly left without their father. John Tobin, Sr., enlisted as a private in the Union Army, specifically the Fifth Regiment, Company K, during the Civil War, and left for his military duty in January 1862.[17] He began his training at Fort Snelling, an army fort in Minnesota, located on a high bluff above the Mississippi River approximately thirty miles southwest of Stillwater.

At the time of John Tobin's enlistment and departure from Stillwater to Fort Snelling, the six Tobin children were the following ages; Richard fourteen, Anna Maria twelve, Margaret seven, John, Jr. four, Cassie three, and James less than one year old. Margaret, the matriarch of the family, would have become the sole caretaker of her children and the boarders who resided with the family when her husband departed for his duties during the Civil War. However, the children may have been left without their mother before he left for his military commitment, or sometime shortly thereafter, as Margaret's name seems to have disappeared from records after the baptism of their youngest child, James in 1861.

The date of when Margaret (Cunningham) Tobin died or where she's laid to rest is unknown, as Washington County didn't begin to record the county deaths until 1870. She was more than likely laid to rest in the early parish's burial grounds, between Third and Fourth Streets north of Laurel in the North Hill area, near where Pioneer Park is located today. In the 1870s, when the early cemetery was becoming overgrown and disheveled, due to lack of care, those who were buried there were re-interred in the newer cemeteries such as Fairview in Stillwater, or St. Michael's in Bayport, Minnesota. If the deceased didn't have a tombstone or grave marker or any other record, before or after their re-interment, finding records or a grave site for them is for the most part impossible.[18]

Regardless of the exact date of when his mother died, Richard, the oldest Tobin child, now had to step up and take on the role of "man of the household" and contribute to looking after the well-being of his five younger siblings due to his father's enlistment. This would have been an enormous undertaking for a young man without much notice of his pending responsibilities, with or without his mother. Future records indicate they also received help from their extended family, the O'Briens.

IN THE NEWS

The Stillwater Messenger, May 3, 1865

By the Governor of Minnesota

Whereas, the President of the United States has, by a proclamation issued by him, appointed and set apart the 1st day of June next, "to be observed wherever in the United States the flag of the country may be respected, as a day of humiliation and mourning," for the death of Abraham Lincoln, our late President…

When children lose parents unexpectedly through death or other circumstances, often they move in with their close relatives.

Sometime before 1870, the Tobin children began to receive support from their extended family, and some began to live with their cousins and their mother's sister and brother-in-law, their aunt Mary Ann and uncle John Felix O'Brien, as listed in Stillwater's 1870 United States Federal Census.

The children adjusted to their new routine with the O'Briens, worshipping during Mass at St. Michael's and attending school with their cousins. Cassie, the youngest Tobin daughter, seemed to do well at school during these turbulent years, as she is one of the many children representing the various grades in the Stillwater schools to have been mentioned in a newspaper article. She is listed in the March 2, 1869, *Stillwater Republican* article as a "Roll of Honor" student, compiled by the superintendent of city schools, J.C. Caldwell. There are several grades listed in the paper that day, mentioning many names in each of the following categories: 1st Intermediate, 2nd Intermediate, Higher Primary, Primary No.1, Primary No. 2, and Primary No. 3, as well as student names from the Schulenburg School.

Cassie Tobin's name appears under the Primary No. 3 section. Her name is listed along with other students, who were no doubt feeling quite special on that day in 1869 to have been mentioned in one of the town's papers.

IN THE NEWS

The Stillwater Republican, March 2, 1869

Roll of Honor—(…) Primary No. 3—Anna Mattison, Mary Register, Emma Register, Lizze O'Donnel, Mary Welch, Ella Foran, Mary Kerr, Cassie Tobin, Lizzie Harrigan, Lizzie Sinclaire, Douglas Greeley, Mary Mackey, Agnes Carle, Lizzie Dudy, Maggie Maragar, Annie Clancy, Annie Clark, Ellen O'Donnel, Maria Parle, Mary Sevine, Mary Chisholm, Lida Jenks, Frank Bromley.

One of the other Tobin children, John, Jr., seemed to have been residing on a farm in Wisconsin during this period. Across the St. Croix, River, in the state of Wisconsin, there's a John Tobin listed as residing with a John Hennesey and family in the town of St. Joseph, according to Wisconsin's 1870 United States Federal Census for the County of St. Croix. This John Tobin is listed as a thirteen-year-old farm laborer and not as a member of the Hennesey family. The age of thirteen would have been the correct age for John, Jr.

If this is the correct John, as a farm laborer in Wisconsin, he would have had to live and work the fields or tend to the animals along with other younger and older men. After an exhausting day, he would have to sleep in a cold and dirty hired hands' bunkhouse.

Without his father, losing his mother at such a young age, and having to move away from his hometown of Stillwater to Wisconsin must have been heart-wrenching for John, Jr., as he continued to mourn the loss of his parents in addition to being separated from his siblings. Did certain memories of his family, living just across the river, run through his mind as he cried himself to sleep each night? How long did it take the young boy to fall asleep while listening to the coughs, sniffles, and snores of his bunkmates? Then, when almost asleep, would he suddenly wake with a jolt, bringing him back to the perpetual nightmare of feeling like a lost and unwanted child?

A few years later, John, Jr. returned to Stillwater. At the age of seventeen he was employed at Isaac Staples's sawmill company.

The Tobin children grew to adulthood without their mother or their father. Their father, John Tobin, Sr., the Irish immigrant and patriarch, who traveled with his small family from Maine to Stillwater in the mid-1850s, was absent for many years after leaving for the Civil War. A short paragraph in the *St. Paul Daily Globe*, dated May 27, 1879, under the "Stillwater News" section states: "John Tobin, an old time resident of Stillwater has returned to the city after an absence of some 14 years . . ." The article goes on to say that he was in the Western States and Territories. As the newspaper article gives his general location during all those years, perhaps he'd been hired by the Union Pacific Railroad company. This was the time when many Irish laborers, including veterans of the Civil War, were hired to lay the tracks for the impending "iron horse," in the western part of the country.[19]

The Trial of Richard Tobin

When researching family history, many people, including myself, put their ancestors upon pedestals. I know of some past family members who belong there. It's easy to think that our ancestors were without fault of any kind and imagine many of them as some sort of saints. What person, of any generation, could not relate to everyday struggles with temptation or personal offenses? After all, we're all human, trying our best each day to overcome our own wrongdoings. Think of today's world, with the overabundance of Internet access, as it lures some individuals toward a variety of unsavory websites and actions with just a click of a button. Time hasn't changed these sorts of human activities, only the way they are acted upon.

When the Tobins arrived in Stillwater in the early 1850s, even before Minnesota was declared a state in the Union, Stillwater was a very small and somewhat primitive town. The streets made of dirt and mud, had saloons and brothels catering to the laborers' and lumbermen's vices.

As the years went on, the Tobin family would have undoubtedly known most of the townspeople, and many of the boarders who resided with them in their home. This makes me wonder: Who were the men in the Tobin boys' lives that influenced and left certain impressions upon them throughout the years. Perhaps it was the lumbermen who came to Stillwater looking for work and lived under the same roof as the Tobins. By day they worked extremely hard in the depths of the woods and upon the river. By night, some would search for the cheapest form of love, comfort, and entertainment from one of the many brothels available to them in St. Paul or within their little logging town, just a few blocks away.[20,21]

There was a particular incident when Richard, the oldest son of John and Margaret Tobin, was accused of a ghastly crime, resulting in a court hearing in 1879. The events that led up to that particular court hearing, involved a Stillwater resident by the name of Mrs. Ellen Wellman, who was indicted for running a house of "ill-fame" in Stillwater.

When Richard was about thirty, he was arrested while in Mrs. Wellman's Stillwater "house of ill-fame." From the newspaper articles I found on this particular event, his visit was not for the usual purpose of visiting that type of establishment. I'm sure if it was, it would have stated so in the papers, as the *St. Paul Daily Globe* provided several articles on this scandalous story between October 3, 1879 and November 27, 1879.

According to an article in the *St. Paul Daily Globe*, dated October 3, 1879, Mrs. Wellman stated that Richard Tobin arrived one evening to her home, located on Fourth Street, along with a young woman who used to live there. According to Mrs. Wellman's testimony printed in the article, Richard asked her if she would allow the young woman to again live with her in her home, to which Mrs. Wellman replied with an immediate and resounding, "No!"

During the hearing, Mrs. Wellman stated that Richard threatened to kill her as soon as she spoke her response to not allow this girl back into her home again. She said an altercation arose after her refusal, and claimed Richard cut her corset with a knife. She stated her life was spared that night due to the steel stay embedded within her corset.

As I continued reading the articles regarding this occurrence, I think there could have been more to the story of what happened that night, due to the outcome of the court hearing. More often than not, there are two sides to a story.

What else could have happened that calamitous night when Richard was arrested? At the time of the altercation, Richard had been a resident of Stillwater for about twenty-four years, arriving with his parents when he was six years old. He knew many of the earlier settlers and residents of Stillwater, and was more than likely very comfortable helping or approaching someone if he felt the need to do so. I don't know the relationship Richard had with the young woman he brought to Mrs. Wellman's house, if any; however, it appears he was trying to help her to move back to where she had been living. When Richard escorted this young woman to the home of Mrs. Wellman and she refused to let her move back into her home, tempers undoubtedly flared. No doubt a scuffle ensued between the parties after her refusal, and things got out of control; perhaps shouting and pushing from the parties was the result. It makes me wonder how the altercation began, and who threatened who first. I find Mrs. Wellman's statement strange, saying that his threat to kill her happened immediately after she had denied the woman shelter in her home. I believe there is much more to the story, details she may have been leaving out to protect herself, as she was a woman running an illegal business—details we may never know.

IN THE NEWS

The St. Paul Daily Globe, November 15, 1879

The jury in the case of the State of Minnesota vs. Richard Tobin rendered the following verdict: We, the jury, find the defendant not guilty in manner and form as charged in the indictment but find him guilty of an assault with a dangerous weapon.

Even though Richard was found not guilty of the intent to do great bodily harm, he was found guilty of assault with a dangerous weapon and sentenced to ninety days in the county jail. As he was only given a ninety-day sentence, it again makes me question if there was more to the story that Richard had revealed during his testimony. Since the State had a doctor as well a policeman testify in court that day, it also makes me wonder if Mrs. Wellman didn't tell the whole version of what happened that night and perhaps the doctor and/or the policeman shed a different light on the whole situation.

A later article in the *St. Paul Daily Globe*, dated November, 20, 1879, states that "the State was represented by County Attorney Thompson." Those who testified on behalf of the State and Mrs. Ellen Wellman were Mrs. Wellman herself, a Dora Wellman, a doctor by the name of Dr. P. H. Millard, a policeman listed as F. S. McKusick, and Delos Hitchcock.

The attorney who represented the defendant, Richard Tobin, was James N. Castle, also known as, J. N. Castle. He was a lawyer from Stillwater who held several prominent positions throughout the years at different times, such as: county attorney, municipal attorney, and a U.S. representative for the state of Minnesota.[22]

Because Richard had been a long-time resident of Stillwater before this event, perhaps he and J.N. Castle were already acquainted with each other before the trial. Either way, Attorney Castle defended Richard's case quite well and was able to get Richard off with just a ninety-day sentence in the county jail.

I also assume that Richard was able to relay his version of the incident to the jury during the court hearing; however, I was unable to locate the court records or any articles regarding his testimony. This, of course, makes me think that there was another side to the story that wasn't fully represented in the newspaper articles during the court hearing in 1879. As we all know, to sell papers, they sometimes have to sensationalize a story.

Mrs. Wellman was also sentenced that day: she was instructed to remove herself from Stillwater. Richard, however, continued to live in his hometown for several more years and is listed in the following years' records as living and being employed as a cook. Richard, being the oldest Tobin child, was the one in charge of his younger siblings for many years after their father's absence and mother's death, and perhaps was used to helping others. However, that's just speculation at this point.

Richard is not my direct ancestor, as he is not a direct-line grandparent, but that of a distant uncle. I want to believe Richard was trying to help correct an unfortunate situation, perhaps to his own detriment. He seemed to have taken on the role as the unplanned leader of his siblings, often being employed as a cook to presumably provide for those who depended on him. He is also listed as the closet family member, living in Stillwater, in the admittance paperwork for his father in 1881, when his father began living at the North-Western Branch National Home for Disabled Vol. Soldiers, in Milwaukee, Wisconsin.[23]

The Tobin Brothers

In 1881, a couple years after Richard's trial, Richard married Emily Gervais of Little Canada, Minnesota, and they eventually moved to Duluth, where he again found employment as a cook. I suppose working at his parents' boarding house all those years prepared him for that particular career.

John, Jr. would also move to Duluth and marry a woman from England, by the name of Mary. Unfortunately, I wasn't able to locate any future records for the youngest Tobin brother, James, born in 1861.

The Tobin Sisters

Two of the Tobin sisters were able to change the course of their destiny to some extent. More details on the lives of Anna Maria and her youngest sister, Catherine (Cassie), will continue in the following chapters. Their sister, Margaret Ellen, still remains a mystery, as she doesn't seem to appear in future records since the 1860 Census record at the age of four.

Acknowledging the Tobin Pioneers

The lives of the first of my ancestors to migrate to Stillwater were probably similar to many families who arrived during the same time, where the children had to witness the death of parents, or parents losing their children, or the struggle children would bear due to some type of family tragedy. The Tobin children would go on to live most of their lives without their parents' love, support, and guidance, while trying to figure out a source of income and the problems of everyday life.

The parents, John and Margaret, no doubt envisioned a totally different life for their family when they left Maine in the mid-1850s. I often wonder if John Tobin, Sr., ever had any regrets about bringing his family to Stillwater after the many incidents of loss and hardship he and his family endured. If his departure from Stillwater to the Western States and Territories for all those years was intentional due to employment, I understand his absence during that time, as I realize his life and the lives of his family had many struggles and difficulties just in getting by from one day to the next.

I believe his journey with his family was not in vain, as I know many of his descendants of our first family of pioneers absolutely love our family origins of Stillwater and its history. Even though their story ends quite sadly for several members of their family, I would want John and Margaret Tobin to know that taking that journey west and persevering throughout all those difficult times is very much appreciated by their descendants. The sacrifices they made to start a new life and begin the family's history as one of the pioneer families of Stillwater, is appreciated by many family members, who love the historic lumber and logging town of our ancestors.

The Tobins arrived around the same time as some of the more prominent and historic men of the town. They left Bangor for Stillwater following on the heels of the ambitious lumbermen from Maine. They were early citizens trying to carve out a new life with the hope of success for their family. Throughout all the challenges and tribulations the earlier settlers had to face in the beginning stages of Stillwater, some families made it and some families didn't. My family's Stillwater history would have been nonexistent if it weren't for the next two groups of ancestors who arrived during the mid-1860s who connected with the Tobins and began my family's legacy.

CHAPTER FOUR

The Wright Family

The Wright Family

<u>Mary Ann Wright* - William Wright*</u>

1822-1896   1821-1857

(2nd Husband J. L. Jones)

1828-1893

<u>Their Children</u>

Addison*

1841-1919

George

1844 - Unknown

Mary Helen

1847 -1931

*Direct Ancestors

"The men were gentlemen and the women were proper."

The Wright surname was spoken in my household very often while I was growing up. The stories and first names regularly attached to this surname were: Addison, Uncle Addy, and mostly Ivy. However, there was another Wright ancestor who settled in Stillwater whom I never heard of while growing up. Not until I was immersed in family history would I discover this family member whom time almost forgot.

Mary Ann Wright, A Name to Remember

The first time I saw Mary Ann's name, it was in the same paperwork with another ancestor's name with whom I was familiar. However, I had no idea who Mary Ann was or how or if I was related to her.

It was a pleasant Minnesota summer day when I traveled a short distance from my home in Afton to Stillwater to do a bit of research. I was on my way to meet with Barbara Bachmeier, the secretary at Fairview Cemetery, as I was planning to visit my great-great-grandfather Addison Wright's grave site for the first time.

After arriving at the Fairview Cemetery office, Barbara located Addison's records and burial information for me and informed me he was buried in the same plot with a Joseph L. Jones and a Mary A. Jones. I was surprised by this and began to wonder if I had the correct Addison Wright. After a brief review of my collected sources, I saw that, yes, I did have the correct Addison Wright, who evidently was laid to rest alongside the Joneses, at Fairview Cemetery.

After Barbara escorted me into the cemetery to pay my respects and take a few photos of Addison's and the Joneses' final resting place, I headed to my next stop, Stillwater Public Library. With Joseph and Mary A. Jones's names and dates of death in hand, I was ready for more research to take on this new challenge.

Upon arriving at the library, I proceeded toward the St. Croix Collection room, which is secured under lock and key. After a staff member unlocked the door, I slowly looked around, orientating myself with the room, which was reminiscent of a barrister's library. The tall bookcases were overflowing with books and periodicals of Stillwater's history. Two large wooden desks with lamps in their centers offered to shed their light and accommodate me during my investigation.

After receiving some instructions, I situated myself in front of the microfilm reader. I began to scroll through the microfilm reel that contained the *Stillwater Gazette*'s January 1896 newspapers, focusing on a date around January 27, 1896, when suddenly . . . I found it! Mary Ann Jones's obituary. As I slowly read each word captured within the ink-smudged copy of "yesteryear's" newspaper, a new revelation began to sink in, and I began to realize I was meeting my great-great-great-grandmother Mary Ann Wright, mother to Addison Wright, for the first time. The details in her obituary had everything I needed to confirm and continue on with my research.

*O*ut of all the distant great-grandparents I heard about while growing up, Mary Ann Wright was never one of them. I heard only stories about her son, Addison, or her grandchildren, Ivy and Addison, Jr. Unfortunately, Mary Ann was somehow forgotten in family history over the years. However, she is one of the ancestors that I have come to know very well due to my research and the abundance of unspoken words about her life.

Mary Ann Wright was said to be vivacious, affectionate, and good-natured, according to a description of her in the ancestral book, *The Wrights of Wright Street,* compiled by distant relatives.[24]

Mary Ann was the eleventh child of sixteen, from her father Christopher's two combined marriages. She was born in her family home on Wright Street in 1822 in Durham, New York, a small town about thirty-five miles southwest of Albany.

Mary Ann's father owned apple orchards and a mill and was therefore able to manufacture cider for the local markets, including his own, from which his income was mostly obtained.

She and her siblings received a good education at the appropriately named Wright Street School, in Greene County, Durham, New York. Her father and some of his brothers founded the school and were also the officials. They opened the school, hired and paid the teachers, organized and moderated the meetings so their children and others in the area could receive a good education.[25] Mary Ann was said to have been a good student and benefited from her education in various ways throughout her life.

In 1840, when she was eighteen years old, she married William Wright, her first cousin-once-removed, who was one year older. William was raised about fifty miles away from where Mary Ann grew up in Greene County. After the two were married, they moved into the home of Mary Ann's parents on Wright Street, where she gave birth to three children in the same place where she herself was born and raised.

Their first child was a son, Addison Wright, born in 1841. Their second child was also a son, named George Wright, who died at a very young age. Lastly, their youngest child was a daughter, Mary Helen Wright, born around 1847.

Shortly after the birth of their daughter, the family began to travel northwest with their two young children, Addison and Mary Helen, and moved away from the family home on Wright Street. Mary Ann left behind her parents, many siblings, and extended family for a very different life from the one she was accustomed to in the little town of Durham.

When Mary Ann's two children were the ages of seventeen and eleven, they suddenly became fatherless, as William died in 1857.

At some point before their move to Stillwater, the small family moved to Chicago where she would meet Joseph L. Jones, also known as J.L. Jones, and they would marry. Her second husband was an accomplished musician and professor of music, who began his training at a very young age.

The Wrights of New York Arrive

The Wrights from New York, whose ancestors originated from England, migrated to Stillwater in the mid-1860s. The men were gentlemen and the women were proper. They were a family who were very well-respected. Mary Ann (Wright) Jones, along with her second husband, Professor Joseph L. Jones, and her two adult children, Addison and Mary Helen, located to Stillwater around 1867.

Mary Ann and Joseph seemed to have had very full and active lives in Stillwater. Their home was located at 515 South Third Street. This particular location was a prominent place to live, sharing the same street with bankers, physicians, and lawyers, who also occupied homes on South Third Street.[26] It was also a perfect place to witness all of the local happenings, as this particular location was known for much activity in Stillwater, as well as being directly across from the courthouse, constructed from 1867 to 1870.

Both Mary Ann and Joseph Jones were involved in service-oriented organizations in Stillwater; namely, the International Order of Odd Fellows and the Daughters of Rebekah, the woman's branch of the Odd Fellows.

During his time with the organization, J.L. Jones held different positions such as "District Deputy Grand Master for the Odd Fellows State of Minnesota Lodge" and the "Chief Patriarch for the Stillwater Lodge."[27]

Musical Roots in the Family Tree

I often wondered how music became such a big part of my family's life throughout the years. When my sisters and I were young, we were all expected to take piano lessons. Even if we didn't want to, it was required. I still love playing the piano and composing music; however, I believe it was the academic practice sessions and exercises of drills and scales that turned me off of having the desire of becoming an accomplished pianist. If I was paying attention to all the details back then, I would have appreciated it more, as I enjoyed listening to both my mother and grandmother when they played their favorite tunes on the piano. Looking back on it now, I wish I would have practiced longer and harder so it wouldn't be such a struggle for me today when sitting down in front of a piece of sheet music for the first time.

Researching my ancestors has given me a greater appreciation for music than when I was a child and fought to escape "tickling the ivories" for thirty to sixty minutes a day. Discovering the deep musical roots in my family has strengthened my drive and given me great joy when learning a new piece of music.

The Music Begins

Mary Ann's second husband, Joseph Jones, was a very talented musician. He served as a musician during the Civil War, in the Fourth Wisconsin Infantry band,[28] and his gift of music continued after the war. He was very active with his musical talent and became a local musician in Stillwater. Professor Jones entertained at a variety of local events, as well as trained the would-be vocalists and instrumentalists of Stillwater. He was also the leader of the Stillwater Cornet Band.[29]

In addition to musical instruction and local performances, he was hired as the church organist and choir director for St. Michael's Catholic Church, which was a short walk away from his home on South Third Street. He held this position with the church for most of his life in Stillwater.

IN THE NEWS

The Stillwater Republican, April 7, 1868

Surprise Party—A pleasant little surprise came off at Mr. Carli's last Monday evening. Jones' string band furnished the music and the company tripped the "light fantastic toe" until the near wee sma' hours, when all returned to their homes feeling as if it was good to be there.

The Stillwater Republican, April 14, 1868

Last Sunday, the finest organ in the city was introduced into Father Murray's (English Catholic) church, and for the first time was used at vespers during the afternoon service. Professor J.L. Jones, an accomplished performer, has been employed as organist and instructor of the choir.

The Stillwater Republican, May 5, 1868

Cornet Band—We are pleased to announce the reorganization of the Stillwater Cornet Band. Last Wednesday evening, the members of the old Band and others met at the office of Durant and Hanford and completed their organization by the election of the following officers:

Leader - Prof J.L. Jones

President - J.R. Carli

Secretary - A.K. Doe

Treasurer - Chas. Kattenburg

A good Band is a large addition to our place and we have no doubt but that they will receive, as they deserve, the encouragement of our citizens.

Music, Balls, and Dancing

During the early years of Stillwater, a favorite activity for the citizens of all ages was to attend public dances and balls held at the many dance halls throughout the town. Some of the more prominent citizens and homeowners of Stillwater would have private ballrooms within their large homes, such as lumber baron Isaac Staples's mansion on the top of the bluff, whose home included a ballroom on the third floor.[30] However, in the early days, the more popular place to hold a dance in Stillwater was at Concert Hall.

The dances and balls were not only for the "older" residents of Stillwater, as the youth of the city enjoyed them just as much. If the families were able to afford to do so, they would hire a dance instructor for their children, something the children would look forward to.[31]

Professor J.L. Jones's band, which included his stepson Addison, would often provide the music during the early years in Stillwater.

IN THE NEWS

The Stillwater, Republican, June 1, 1869

Social Ball—A social ball will be given to-morrow evening at Concert Hall. Music will be furnished by Professor Jones' string band.

The Stillwater Republican, November 2, 1869

Thanksgiving Dance—We learn that the young men about town propose getting up a social hop on Thanksgiving evening on Nov 18, in Concert Hall. An oyster supper will be furnished at the Minnesota House. Music by Prof. Jones' Band.

The Stillwater, Republican, November 9, 1869

The Germans of this city will give a ball at Concert Hall, Friday evening, November 26, 1869.

Music by Prof. Jones' Band

Supper at Minnesota House

Everybody is invited

The Stillwater Republican, January 18, 1870

The Universalists will henceforth hold their social hops every Wednesday evening. Music by Jones' Band. Dancing commences at 8 o'clock and closes precisely at 11.

Mary Ann's Son, Addison Wright

Shortly after Addison's arrival in Stillwater with his mother, Mary Ann, stepfather, J.L. Jones, and sister, Mary Helen, he became a journeyman and trained to be a licensed painter. He went on to become a co-owner of painting businesses in Stillwater. His first partnership was with Smith and Webster, known as Smith, Webster and Wright; he also became a partner with B.J. Mosier, known as Wright and Mosier, among others. Even though the partnership names changed from time to time from when he first embarked on that business, being a painter would become his lifelong profession.[32]

Addison was part of the music corp during the Civil War, and would play both brass and string instruments. He became proficient on string instruments—specifically his fiddle, which is what he is remembered for by his descendants. After the Civil War and moving to Stillwater, he was a member of the cornet band with his stepfather.

Addison was involved in different bands and orchestra organizations in Stillwater, along with Professor Jones, and would entertain publicly or privately for family and friends on different occasions, and for the townspeople of Stillwater throughout the years.

Mary Ann's Daughter, Mary Helen Wright

Shortly after arriving to Stillwater, Mary Ann's daughter, Mary Helen, met and married a man by the name of Charles Kattenburg. Mary Helen's husband, Charles, was also a musician and member of the cornet band, along with her brother, Addison Wright, and stepfather J.L. Jones.

Mary Helen and her husband, Charles, had one daughter together by the name of Grace Kattenburg, born in 1869.

Grand Masquerade and Fancy-Dress Ball

IN THE NEWS

The Stillwater Republican, February 15, 1870,

Grand

Masquerade

and

Fancy Dress

Ball,

Concert Hall

at

Stillwater,

Friday, eveni'g Feb. 25th, 1870

he advertisement for the Masquerade and Fancy Dress Ball, reserved for February 25th, 1870, gave all the details for the upcoming evening's events. Tickets to the ball were $2.00, supper at the Sawyer House were $1.00, and those who wanted to enjoy the evening's events as spectators would pay $.50 for entrance into the venue. The advertisement also stated that sleighs would be in attendance to convey persons to and from the hall.

Four days after the Masquerade Ball, *The Stillwater Republican*, on March 1, 1870, reported on the details of the successful event. The article states it was "one of the most successful and pleasant dances of the season, and the costumes were by far the richest ever worn." Over forty couples were enjoying the night's events, along with many spectators. It also states within the article that, "Jones' band furnished the music, for this very successful and enjoyable ball."

Some of the guests, and the costumes that were donned that evening were: "I. E. Staples representing Don Cesar de Bazan in a Brigand suit of rich material, and his wife was dressed as 'Folly'... Joe Carli was dressed as the Man with the Iron Mask. Miss Emma Nelson and Miss Mary Davis were Vivandeers. Mr. Charles Kattenburg was a 'clown' and Mrs. and Miss Kattenburg wore fancy dresses."

Others in attendance included: Mr. Charles Staples, dressed first as the 15th Amendment, then later, the Earl of Essex; Miss Olivia Staples and Miss Levi Proctor were Swiss peasants; Miss Ada Lowell wore a fancy dress; Mrs. C.N. Nelson was a Scotch Lassee; Mr. A.K. Doe was dressed as a Cavalier and his wife was dressed as a Nun; and Mr. S. Carli was an Army Surgeon. A couple of the out-of-town guests from St. Paul wore Zouave costumes.

The article names many more attendees and their costumes and also states that there were quite a number of other guests present that were not mentioned in the article, "but the whole was a most pleasant affair."

CHAPTER FIVE

Addison and Anna Maria

Anna Maria Tobin Becomes a Wright

Anna Maria Tobin was the oldest daughter of John and Margaret Tobin, the first of my family of early pioneers to locate to Stillwater in the mid-1850s. She met Addison Wright, who was eight years her senior, within a couple years after he located to Stillwater in the mid-1860s. I often wonder how they met. Did Addison meet Anna Maria at a town dance, where he and his stepfather provided music, or a special celebration the city organized for its residents? Perhaps he met Anna Maria at St. Michael's church, where her family attended and Addison's stepfather was employed as the musical director. Perhaps they met through mutual friends, or one of Anna Maria's O'Brien cousins. It could have been any one of these scenarios. I like to imagine each of them when I think of their first encounter within the charming town.

Before Addison and Anna Maria were married, he signed a legal document, on August 4, 1869, to purchase property from William Webster, Mortimer Webster, and his wife Annie Webster, to build a home in a neighborhood called "the Webster's Addition." For the amount of $125, Addison purchased from the Webster's lot number five (5) and the first half of lot number Four (4), as surveyed and platted by H.C. Shepard, Esq., per the document.

The following year, in May 1870, Addison and Anna Maria were married. After their marriage, while Addison and Anna Maria were having their house built in the Webster's Addition, they lived with Addison's mother and her husband; a servant named Ellen Peterson was also an occupant and domestic help at the home of the Joneses during that time.

Addison and Anna Maria's new home, located at 518 West Olive Street, was just a few blocks away from where the first courthouse in Stillwater, as well as in Minnesota, used to be located on Chestnut and Fourth Streets.[33]

Anna Maria Tobin,
circa 1870
Tin Type Photograph
Courtesy of Jon Meister

Addison Wright,
circa 1870
Tin Type Photograph
Courtesy of Jon Meister

Their Legacy Begins

The year 1871 was a milestone year for Addison and Anna Maria. Just after having their home completed, they welcomed their first child, a son they named, Addison, Jr. His godparents, listed on his baptism records from St. Michael's Catholic Church, were his mother's cousin, Margaret O'Brien, and his mother's brother, Richard Tobin (whose arrest and court hearing would occur eight years later).

IN THE NEWS

The Stillwater Messenger, May 19, 1871

A new stairway is being built on Chestnut Street, leading from Third Street to the old Court House hill.

The Stillwater Messenger, June 2, 1871

Thermometer indicated 90 above Wednesday at noon in the shade. We shall have few better days this summer.

St. Michael's Church—The Cornerstone Laid

Two years later, when Addison and Anna Maria were on the cusp of welcoming their second child into the world, a beautiful, holy, and historic event took place for St. Michael's Catholic Parish.

IN THE NEWS

The Stillwater Messenger, Friday June 27, 1873

St. Michael's Church

THE CORNERSTONE LAID—AN IMPRESSIVE CEREMONY—1,000 VISITORS FROM ST. PAUL, MINNEAPOLIS AND HASTINGS—NEARLY 2,000 PERSONS IN PROCESSION

Last Sunday was a gala day for the Catholics of Stillwater, for it was the occasion of the formal ceremony of laying the cornerstone of the magnificent new Church on the corner of Third and Walnut Streets for St. Michael's Parish.

This ceremonious event for the parishioners of St. Michael's was held on Sunday, June 22, 1873. The occasion was attended by many clergy and a variety of Catholic societies from St. Paul, Minneapolis, and Hastings. The historic event celebrated by Stillwater citizens, Catholic or otherwise, began with the Stillwater Cornet Band marching from the old church, at Fourth and Mulberry Streets, to the train depot where they welcomed their out-of-town guests who would be joining the band for a procession to the old church, and then on to the new church for its cornerstone ceremony and benediction.

When the guests exited the train cars at the depot and were arranged accordingly, the procession began, with the Stillwater Cornet Band in the lead. The visiting guests proceeded along with them to the old church at

Fourth Street. After they arrived at the old church, Bishop Grace read Low Mass. The old church was completely full, with standing-room-only worshippers, as well as many remaining outside.

At the conclusion of Mass, the procession formed again and proceeded to march through the streets of Stillwater toward the site of the new church at Third and Walnut Streets. Following the Stillwater Cornet Band, the procession participants were organized in the following order:

Council of Catholic Union,

St. Vincent de Paul organizations from;

The Cathedral of St. Paul

St. Mary's of St. Paul

Stillwater

Minneapolis

Hastings

Emerald Cornet Band, Minneapolis

Irish Rifles, Minneapolis

St. Peter Benevolent Society (German) St. Paul

St. Boniface Benevolent Society (German) Hastings

Father Matthew T.A.S., Minneapolis

Father Matthew T.A.S., St. Paul

St. Joseph's T.A.S., St. Paul

National Band

Temperance Crusaders, St. Paul

Stillwater Band

Temperance Crusaders, Stillwater

St. Patrick's Society, Stillwater

Young Boys C.A., Stillwater

Holy Angel's Sodality, Stillwater

The last of the procession participants to arrive at the new site was the Holy Angel's Sodality of Stillwater. They led the small procession into the church building site, beginning with Bishop Grace and followed by the attending clergy to begin the ceremonies. The ceremony included an address by Father Ireland of the St. Paul Cathedral and special prayers and blessings by Bishop Grace, with the assistance of St. Michael's pastor, Father Murphy, as well as Father Ireland and Father Goiffin.

The procession that day was said to have been more than a mile long, with nearly 2,000 participants. This was truly a joyous occasion in the history of Stillwater, the building of a holy space that would become the worshiping home to many Stillwater families for generations to come. The church was completed two years later, in 1875.

Ivy Maria Wright Is Born

*J*ust two days after the historic laying of the cornerstone at St. Michael's Catholic Church, Addison and Anna Maria welcomed their second child, my future great-grandmother Ivy Maria Wright, born on June 24, 1873. Ivy's godparents are listed as her mother's sister, Catherine (Cassie) Tobin, and her mother's cousin, James F. O'Brien. The two young godparent cousins were only fourteen and twelve years old, respectively.

Even though Ivy's father, Addison, was not Catholic, he agreed with his wife, Anna Maria, to have their children baptized and raised Catholic. The Wrights came from a long line of Presbyterians in New York, including Addison's great-grandfather, George Wright, who was a deacon in the Greenville Presbyterian Church.[34] However, Addison knew his wife was raised Catholic at St. Michael's Parish, beginning in the 1850s, and they were now residents of Stillwater starting a family of their own.

The couple seemed to be doing quite well for themselves in Stillwater. Addison, the sole provider of the family and co-proprietor of a painting shop also enjoyed entertaining the locals with his musical abilities. They had a life that many families begin with; a boy, a girl and adoring parents.

The first couple of years of their daughter Ivy's life was that of any typical young infant and toddler. She had an older brother and two loving parents. I suspect that they had many family and friends over to their Olive Street home to welcome their new baby girl, as many extended family and friends lived in homes walking distance from their home on Olive Street. They were close enough for Anna Maria to make the short walk with her children to visit with her aunt Mary Ann and uncle John F. O'Brien and cousins, as well as her sister Cassie, who was residing with them at 320 North Second Street. During weekly shopping trips, I imagine, Anna Maria would stop by the paint shop with the children to visit with her husband, as their children tested the paint samples with their little fingers and small brushes.

The organizations of Stillwater continued with their high-spirited activities, celebrating holidays and special occasions for the small-town residents, which the young family would enjoy.

An Unexpected Day, September 1875

Autumn is such a beautiful time of year in Minnesota, a favorite among the locals. It's a time of year that creates such beauty it can make anyone stop and admire the greatness of God's creative abilities. The summer's humidity finally drifts away, leaving a subtle cool crispness in the air as brightly colored leaves fall slowly, traveling toward their final resting place.

On September 7, 1875, Addison, the thirty-four-year-old father, along with four-year-old son, Addison, Jr., and two-year-old daughter, Ivy, were dressed in their Sunday's best for a Tuesday church service when they departed their Olive Street home.

Preparing a four- and two-year-old for a long day was a new challenge for Addison, as his wife, Anna Maria, was the one who clothed the children in their outfits each day.

After their arrival at the church and greeting many family and friends, the somber services began and lasted about an hour. After the services came to a close, the procession to the cemetery was the largest the city had seen in many a year.

Addison, the newly widowed father, would now have to come to terms with being a single father to his two young children. Addison wasn't the only father who was heart-broken that day from a recent loss. He and fellow Stillwater citizen, Duncan Chisholm, became connected throughout time due to the grief-stricken day they shared in 1875.

IN THE NEWS

The Lumberman Newspaper, September 10, 1875

On Monday Mrs. A.M. Wright, wife of Addison Wright, and Mrs. Chisholm, wife of the policeman, died. They were both highly esteemed ladies and leave families of small children behind.

Their funerals took place together last Tuesday, the remains being escorted to the graves by one of the largest funeral processions seen in the city for many a year.

The Minneapolis Tribune, September 7, 1875

Monday, at 4 A.M. Mrs. Addison Wright died on Court House hill, after a brief illness. Mr. W. is well known here as a painter and musician and at this time has the heartfelt sympathies of the entire community in his deep affliction . . .

Mrs. Chisholm, the other woman who was being mourned that day, was the wife of Duncan Chisholm. At the untimely death of his wife, he was a police officer in Stillwater. He also held the position of chief of police at different times for the city.[35]

Mrs. Chisholm died shortly after giving birth to their youngest child, a daughter. Officer Chisholm would now also be the sole caretaker to his children, including the infant daughter his wife had given birth to a few days prior to her funeral—this daughter lived into adulthood.

When imagining a procession in Stillwater, I think of Fourth of July parades, or the town's recent St. Michael's Church procession that filled the streets with joy just two years prior, in 1873. Because some of the children of the two deceased mothers were so young, I wonder what their behavior was like during the procession. Did they think they were in a parade as they proceeded to the cemetery that day, traveling along to the cemetery toward the unknown destination that would become all too familiar?

When people die at such a young age, in the prime of their lives, it always makes me think of the phrase "what could have been." It's a phrase that accompanies these tragic events that become a continuous and heartbreaking thread throughout generations of family history.

When Addison, a native of New York, and resident of Stillwater for just under ten years, stood at his wife's grave that day, was he flooded with memories of his dear Anna Maria, and the stories she had told him about her and her family's arrival to the logging town of Stillwater?

During the few years Addison and Anna Maria had together, she would tell her husband that her family were early settlers to Stillwater arriving in the mid-1850s, several years before Addison's arrival. He would make sure his children knew their mother's story, and her family's pioneer beginnings. The stories would be told to their descendants for generations to come.

When It Rains, It Pours

I think many people have heard the phrase, "when it rains it pours" at least once in their lives. When something bad or unfortunate happens, another unfortunate event occurs on the heels of the first one.

It had only been two months since Addison's wife Anna Maria died when the paint shop he was co-owner of, Smith, Wright and Mosier, was hit with a tragedy.

IN THE NEWS

The Stillwater Messenger November 19, 1875

LANDMARKS WIPED OUT.

FIRE TUESDAY EVENING—BROMLEY'S LIVERY STABLE DESTROYED—ALSO FITZGERALD'S BLACKSMITH SHOP AND SALOON—AND SMITH, WRIGHT and MOSIER'S PAINT SHOP— NARROW ESCAPE OF THE MINNESOTA HOUSE AND MUCH OTHER PROPERTY.

Shortly after eight o'clock last Tuesday evening the fire alarm was sounded, when a bright light was discovered near Bromley's livery stable. Reaching the ground it was found that Fitzgerald and Ryan's Blacksmith shop was in flames, and unless the fire was speedily extinguished Bromley's livery stable would be swept away, in which event, owing to a by no means gentle breeze from W.N.W. it seemed quite probable that the Minnesota House and many adjoining buildings would be burned, when there was every reason to believe that a general conflagration would ensue.

The fire engine, hose carts and hook and ladder trucks were promptly in position, and were soon doing effective work . . .

The more valuable articles in Smith, Wright and Mosier's paint shop were removed before this building was in flames . . .

The article continues with the heading "LOSSES AND INSURANCE," stating each establishment's losses from the fire. Addison Wright, along with the co-owners of the paint shop, were able to rebuild and continued forward with their business. Their losses were much less than the other establishments, theirs being between $150 to $200. The losses experienced by Fitzgerald and Ryan's blacksmith shop were approximately $750, Fitzgerald's saloon's losses were figured to be around $400. None of the above-mentioned shops had insurance to cover any of their damages. The only business that carried an insurance policy was Bromley's livery stable. His insurance was in the amount of $1500. His plans for rebuilding were estimated to be in the amount of $2500, therefore his losses were estimated to be no more than $1000.

CHAPTER SIX

Addison Perseveres

Addison continued to raise his children, Addison, Jr., and Ivy, as a single father in his home on Olive St. Because of the demands of his painting business or the opportunities as a musician that were presented from time to time, Addison needed assistance to care for his young children. I believe he had some help from his mother or his late wife's family, the Tobins, and the O'Brien cousins, to relieve him of his single-parent duties on occasion. Addison's late wife's sister, Cassie Tobin, who was still living with her O'Brien relatives, was only sixteen when her sister, Anna Maria, died—the perfect age to babysit and help care for her motherless niece and nephew.

A New Year to Look Forward To

I'm sure Addison was very much looking forward to the start of a new year after experiencing the hardships of 1875.

From the looks of an article dated January 7, 1876 in the *Stillwater Messenger*, it appears the Stillwater residents of the past enjoyed much merriment and celebration on New Year's Eve, as much as current-day residents.

On New Year's Eve, 1875, Mr. and Mrs. Myron Shepard and Mr. and Mrs. John J. Robertson hosted a gathering, at Hersey and Staples Hall. An estimated total amount of guests attending were between 300 and 400 ladies and gentlemen, "and the number present seemed to demonstrate that they had a large number of 'friends.'"

New Year's Eve is an occasion to celebrate during any generation. An evening where the ladies, and gentlemen, look their best and perhaps try to "outdo" one another with their particular attire. In 1875, for a special evening such as this, the women would wear evening gowns, which differed from their day wear, as during the day the necklines would be higher. The evening gown necklines in 1875 were often slightly more revealing than the day dresses. The women would accessorize their bare necks with choker necklaces, some more extravagant than others. A choker necklace could be as simple as a ribbon with a single pendant dangling in the middle, or a fringe necklace made of several jewels or pearls adorning the neck.

The gowns still had an abundance of fabric, but it was in a draping style, sometimes with several layers of fabric in the front of the gown, and at times decorated with large fabric bows, more often in the back. The style was also becoming more trimmed with a straighter appearance, still cinched at the waist with a corset, and included a bustle in the back. Although bustles were still an accessory worn by the ladies at that time, they were becoming a bit smaller in size.

Their formal footwear worn during that era were called a dress slipper or a clog. These formal shoes, made of brightly colored satin, had chunky, one to two-inch heels, and would be embellished with beads or embroidery. To finish off their ensemble, the women would make sure to bring their evening gloves with them, which were an important fashion accessory to present a proper appearance. The gloves were usually about halfway to the elbow. Some women may have brought an extra pair in case the first set became a bit unclean.

The men's attire during a formal occasion would include basic black trousers and a basic white shirt, which would be topped off with a detachable collar and cuffs, as laundering their shirts wasn't as common during that era as it is today. Their possibly "dirty" shirt, with detachable collar and cuffs, would then be covered by a vest, or waistcoat, to give them a neat appearance. To accessorize the basic white shirt, the men would wear bow ties or ascots, popular during the Victorian era. Their shoes for a formal occasion were similar to black leather Oxford shoes or black leather ankle-high boots, sometimes with a pair of spats covering them. To finish off their formal attire, the men's coats would be trim and slim-fitting, the length falling just above the knee. A black top hat and cane would finish off their ensemble before they left for the event of the evening.

According to the January 7, 1876, article, the Germania Orchestra, including Addison Wright and his fiddle, were the musicians who furnished the music for the conclusion of 1875, and welcomed in the Centennial New Year. The article states:

"Shortly after 10 o'clock the members of the Germania Orchestra took position on the stage and Ad. Wright commenced his chin music, when the greater portion of the spacious hall was filled with merry dancers."

There were also tables set up for those who, instead of dancing, would rather play cards, such as whist and euchre. Shortly before midnight, there was an assortment of food and drink and a collection of delicious appetizers to choose from for the guests to enjoy. At this time, the women would usually remove their gloves so to take in something to eat. After everyone had reached their fill of the palatable snacks, many gentlemen adjourned to another room to engage in conversation and to sample the contents of several cigar boxes. When they returned to the hall, the music resumed and the dancing began once again.

"Leave-taking commenced shortly before 2 o'clock, and it was after 3 o'clock before the last guests bid their hosts good morning with wishes for their happiness during the year which had been ushered in."

I would imagine Addison felt a sense of renewal at the stroke of midnight on that New Year's Eve. It was time to leave 1875 behind and move forward to care for himself and his two small children.

Addison Wright, Jr., circa 1877
Tin Type Photograph
Courtesy of Jon Meister

Ivy Maria Wright, circa 1877
Tin Type Photograph Courtesy
of Jon Meister

Addison's New Life

After Addison's wife died, perhaps her sister, Cassie Tobin, aunt to Addison's children and godmother to his daughter, Ivy, felt it was her duty to continue to look after her sister's children. Addison and Cassie must have spent a good amount of time together caring for his youngsters, as the two were eventually married in 1879, four years after the death of Anna Maria. Cassie was twenty years old at the time of her marriage to Addison. He was thirty-eight, being eighteen years her senior. Their marriage took place on May 2, 1879, with Byron J. Mosier and Cassie's cousin, Maggie A. O'Brien, as their attendants.

Cassie's father, John Tobin, Sr., moved into the house on Olive Street, along with Cassie, Addison, and Addison's two small children. John, Sr., was already the children's maternal grandfather through his eldest daughter, Anna Maria. He had recently returned to Stillwater that same year (1879), after a long absence in the Western States and Territories. He lived with Cassie and her new family for a short while, until he moved to a veteran's home for disabled soldiers in Milwaukee, Wisconsin, in 1881.

Addison's second wife added some needed joy to the household on Olive Street, bringing new life when she gave birth to several more children. She had five children during her marriage to Addison. Their first three children were named, according to their births: Margaret Lee, born in 1880; Mary Ann, born in 1882; and George Cleveland, born in 1885.

Addison continued to include music in his children's lives, as eldest son, Addison, Jr., also became very proficient on the fiddle. In later years, Addison, Jr., would accompany his father to different events to perform for the residents of Stillwater.

The Past Is Found in the Present

When I connected with the recent-day owners of Addison's home at 518 West Olive Street, Dave and Beth, they offered my sister and me a tour of their historic, newly renovated home. I could tell by their smiles and welcoming attitude that they loved hearing about our great-great-grandfather Addison Wright as much as we loved hearing about his home, the secrets it may contain, and the details of its renovation.

When we began our tour, after walking up the several steps to the porch that leads to the entrance of the home, I noticed a small wooden sign attached to the exterior of the sky-blue home, to the right of the front door. The sign was painted white, approximately 12 inches in length, and 8 inches in width, with my great-great-grandfather's name and the year 1871 written on it in black lettering: *Addison Wright 1871*. Beth explained to me that where she is from on the East Coast, it's a common practice to place this type of plaque on your home to honor the original homeowner, including the year the home was built.

After slowly touring their home, taking in every room, I imagined my ancestors entering and exiting, and Addison's children running up and down the narrow staircase, with its sharp right turn, to and from the bedrooms on the upper level. The biting freeze they must have felt when slowly walking down the steep steps into the root cellar to retrieve their stored produce and canned goods during the cold Minnesota winter months, must have been more than chilly. When I finally brought myself back to present time, the homeowners were excited to show us a secret treasure they found hidden away for many years within the walls of their home.

During the renovation of the house, they found, hidden behind a wall in an upper room, tucked safely away among the home's original "insulation" of newspapers and horse hair, a very old school book, published in 1885 by Wentworth and Reed, entitled *First Steps in Numbers A Primary Arithmetic, Pupils Edition.* They seemed almost apologetic of the book's rough shape when showing it to us, as it was very aged, and the book's threaded seam, binding it together, had slowly loosened over the years. However, for being over 134 years old from its publishing date and being hidden behind a wall for well over 100 years, its condition wasn't too bad.

***First Steps in Numbers A Primary Arithmetic, Pupils Edition*
*Image Courtesy of Beth and Dave Rogers***

There are a couple names written within the pages of the book, a Matie Wright, which was the nickname given to Addison and Cassie's daughter, Margaret, and the name Cleveland Wright, Addison and Cassie's youngest son. A hand-written message penned by Cleveland is also written in the pages of the book.

Cleveland's message was apparently addressed to his "dearest friend." The following group-deciphered message of warning, including the typos, by Cleveland Wright reads as follows:

Do not steal this book my dearest friend for fear it will be

your end and when you died the lord will say where is that

book you stole away and if you say I do not no up the ladder

and down the rope and their you hang until you choke.

Written by

Cleveland Wright

Stillwater

Minne

Such a message lost in time, that even in today's world would put any young recipient on high alert.

Children throughout all of history are basically the same: innately mischievous, with immature antics and sibling rivalry; a never-ending tradition in all family households, no matter what the era.

CHAPTER SEVEN

The Bells of St. Michael's

A New Responsibility

$\mathscr{I}$n 1883, St. Michael's parishioners were anxiously awaiting the arrival and installation of a set of 10 new chime bells for the church's bell tower. Before the bells were installed, they were blessed on the front lawn of the church, witnessed by the onlooking parishioners.

IN THE NEWS

The Stillwater Messenger, July 21, 1883

The ceremony of blessing the chime bells will take place at St. Michael's church to-morrow, commencing at ten o'clock.

The chime bells for St. Michael's church arrived Monday. They will be hung as soon as parties from the factory arrive for the purpose.

After the church bells were installed in St. Michael's bell tower, J.L. Jones became the first resident bell chimer for the newly installed set of 10 church bells. To demonstrate the operation of the bells, a Professor Mellon from Baltimore came to Stillwater to instruct Professor Jones on the intricacies involved.[36]

After their installation, the training for Professor Jones's additional responsibility commenced. The new task was said to be very exhausting.

Professor Jones would pull the ropes to ring the bells to signal the upcoming Masses each day. The bells were also rung every day to remind the

Catholics of the city to pray the Angelus, which traditionally is three times a day, at six o'clock in the morning, noon, and one more time at six o'clock in the evening. There were other times when Professor Jones would ring out to the city a variety of songs and hymns throughout the year. During the Christmas season, I imagine him ringing out a variety of carols that echoed from the bell tower for the citizens to enjoy while strolling through town during a light winter snowfall.

However, the novelty of the new church bells was apparently wearing off for some residents just a couple years after their installation, as there were some complaints. One complaint appeared in the April 4, 1885, *Stillwater Messenger*: "If church bells can be kept quiet during the last three days of Lent out of respect for the dead, why can they not be kept quiet during the rest of the year out of respect for the living?"

Hopefully Professor Jones didn't take those types of complaints and comments too personally, as he was only performing the job he was hired and trained to do. Even though J.L. Jones wasn't Catholic, he was a dedicated musician and employee of St. Michael's Catholic Church during most of his life in Stillwater.

CHAPTER EIGHT

Cassie

History Repeats Itself

Cassie (Tobin) Wright, formally known as Catherine, gave birth to two additional infant daughters, in 1891 and 1892. Sadly, both infants died shortly after their births, a common event during that time. Her last child, born in April 1892, lived less than twenty-four hours. In a woeful turn of events, Addison was then reminded of a painful loss many years prior, when history repeated itself.

Just six days after his infant daughter's death in 1892, Addison's second wife, Cassie, died of complications of Bright's Disease. Cassie and both of her infant daughters who died one after the other in 1891 and 1892, are all laid to rest together at St. Michael's Cemetery in Bayport, Minnesota, in the plot owned by her O'Brien relatives, near her aunt, uncle, and cousins. It's obvious that the O'Brien relatives were constant supporters of their Tobin nieces and nephews throughout the years, as they were the ones who welcomed them into their home after their father's absence and the death of their mother. In 1859, Cassie Tobin also shared her baptism day with her infant cousin, Martin, who died shortly thereafter.

Once again, the O'Briens were there to support Addison as they saw Cassie and her infant daughter laid to rest near Cassie's cousin, Martin Thomas O'Brien, whom she shared a holy moment in time with thirty-three years prior.

Addison found himself as a widower for a second time and was again left alone to raise his children. I'm sure a flood of memories must have overwhelmed him at the thought of the loss of Anna Maria, who died seventeen years earlier.

At the time of Cassie's death, the ages of her and Addison's children were: Margaret, twelve, Mary Ann, ten, and Cleveland, seven. Addison's older children from his first wife were Addison, Jr., twenty, and Ivy, eighteen. Ivy assisted her father in the care of her younger half-siblings. Addison, Jr. had recently married a woman named Mary Mollie McGee, in Hudson, Wisconsin, just two months prior to Cassie's death.

IN THE NEWS

The Stillwater Gazette, April 12, 1892,

Cassie, wife of Addison Wright, died this morning, from troubles brought on by Bright's disease. The deceased was 33 years old and leaves a husband and three children to mourn her departure.

*T*he days spent raising his young children as a twice-widowed bachelor would have undoubtedly kept Addison's mind off the most difficult of memories that would preoccupy his mind from time to time. Addison continued with his business as an owner of the paint shop, as well as with his music, performing with his stepfather, Professor Jones, while continuing to care for his children.

CHAPTER NINE

The Joneses

Professor J.L. Jones

Professor Jones spent many years of a life full of hustle and bustle in Stillwater, with his responsibilities at St. Michael's, his service organizations, and his home filled with daily musical compositions that he shared with the community. His music suddenly ended for the town of Stillwater when he died of pneumonia on June 16, 1893, at the age of sixty-five.

IN THE NEWS

The St. Paul Daily Globe, June 18, 1893

Stillwater News

Death of Prof. J.L. Jones

Professor J.L. Jones who has been ill with pneumonia the past fortnight, died late Friday night at his home at South Third Street. Deceased came to Stillwater about 27 years ago and was prominent in musical circles. He was a member of the local lodge of Odd Fellows, and was a hard worker in the interest of the lodge.

The Minneapolis Tribune, June 18, 1893,

Obituary

Professor J.L. Jones

Stillwater, Minn.—June 17, [Special] Professor J.L. Jones a prominent resident of Stillwater, died last night of pneumonia. He was a leading member of the Stillwater lodge of Odd Fellows and was 65 years old.

During the days of Professor Jones's illness and subsequent death, the church bells of St. Michael's would have undoubtedly been silent.

One year after his death, Mary Ann purchased three cemetery plots at Fairview Cemetery in Stillwater and had her husband re-interred in one of the newly purchased plots.

The Woman from New York

The only story I know that could have been about Mary Ann (Wright) Jones was a brief story my mother remembered hearing many years ago. The story was that there was a woman in the family who moved to Stillwater from New York and would often entertain and host parties. Mary Ann and her husband, Joseph, lived on South Third Street directly across from the courthouse. Those who lived on South Third hosted festive social events and fashionable weddings. As accomplished musicians, her husband and son Addison, undeniably enjoyed the entertainment business. They played their music for a variety of dances and private parties beginning shortly after their arrival in Stillwater. Being that the Joneses lived on South Third Street, the busy street of well-to-do citizens, I assume the couple hosted private parties, and Joseph and Addison gladly entertained their guests.[37]

After reviewing her life and related information, I believe the woman briefly spoken of to my mother was my three-times great-grandmother, Mary Ann (Wright) Jones, whose name was somehow forgotten during conversations about our Stillwater family history.

IN THE NEWS

The Stillwater Gazette

Stillwater, Minn., Wednesday, January 29, 1896

Death of a Septuagenarian

Mrs. Mary A. Jones died from a stroke of paralysis this morning between 2 and 3 o'clock at her residence, 515 South Third Street. She had been in very feeble health for several years, having suffered two paralytic attacks during that time. It is a consolation to her relatives and friends to know that her death was painless. She appeared in her usual health on Saturday and went out riding on that day in company with her daughter, Mrs. W. J. Harper. Between 11 and 12 o'clock that night, Mrs. Harper went to her mother's room and in answer to her inquiry, remarked, "I am feeling real well." These were her last words. On Sunday morning, Mrs. Jones was found to be in a comatose condition and although a physician was speedily summoned, she never regained consciousness.

Mrs. Jones was born in Green county N.Y. In 1822. Her first husband was William A. Wright, father of the two children of the deceased, Addison Wright and Mrs. W.J. Harper.

She was married to J.L. Jones about 30 years ago. Mr. Jones died in June 1893.

The funeral will occur from the family residence Wednesday afternoon at 2:30, and will be conducted by the Daughters of Rebekah, of which society deceased was a honored member.

Her Final Wishes

The contents of Mary Ann's will are somewhat telling as to who this ancestor, and three-times great-grandmother of mine from New York, was. When I read her will, the first thing that stood out to me was her request to have her heirs erect a prominent tombstone or monument, with the appropriate inscription thereon, in Stillwater's Fairview Cemetery in memory of her and her late husband, Professor J.L. Jones. The aged, white-obelisk-type monument in Stillwater's Fairview Cemetery stands approximately four feet tall.

The largest percentage of the sale of her house at 515 South Third Street went to her son Addison. The percentage totaled $600, equivalent to over $16,500 today. Addison also inherited a bed and all its bedding. Mary Ann's daughter, Mary Helen, who married William J. Harper after her divorce from Charles Kattenburg, received a smaller percentage of $200, which is equivalent to over $5,500 today, as well as the rest her mother's furnishings and household goods. In addition, Mary Ann (Wright) Jones's granddaughter, Grace Kattenburg, received a fur cloak.

Remembering Mary Ann

Mary Ann (Wright) Jones, the ancestor that no one spoke of for several generations, had a life that my family and I missed out on hearing about over the years; however, I am happy to bring her story and that of her second husband, Joseph L. Jones, into existence for family, friends, and readers, to know about their lives during the early days of Stillwater.

I close this chapter with my thoughts on what Mary Ann's life may have been like throughout the years, through the discoveries of my research presented by unspoken words.

Her spirit came alive to me as I imagined her growing up on Wright Street in Greene County, New York. I imagine her and her siblings running cheerfully through their father's apple orchard, climbing trees to help their father pick and harvest the family's commodity, climbing the last tree to be harvested as she tried to reach the highest apple that so stubbornly remained out of reach, even with the strongest shake of the branch it's attached to. I get the sense she would be at the top of her class, competing with her sisters and cousins in a spelling bee, in the little schoolhouse her father and uncles established for the local children in Durham.

I understand how she felt leaving her parents and family behind when she and her small family left New York, never to move back to the home of her birth on Wright Street.

Her life in Stillwater always brings a smile to my face as I imagine her living across the street from the stately courthouse, her involvement with local organizations, shopping on Main Street, hosting parties, and being the proud wife of a local professor of music in her small adopted town.

Rest in peace, Grandmother Mary Ann. I will remember you and share your almost forgotten legacy.

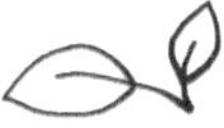

CHAPTER TEN

The McLaggan Family

The McLaggan Family

Kenneth W. McLaggan* m. Rebecca McRae*

1835 - 1900   1838 - 1913

Their Children

John Alexander*

1865 - 1953

Kenneth W., Jr.

1868 - 1938

Eva Rebecca

1871 - 1932

Roderick Hugh

1874 - 1935

*Direct Ancestors

"The McLaggans were a strong, proud, and hard working Scottish family with high moral values and integrity."

This family from Stillwater are the ancestors I learned the most about at an early age, as my maternal grandmother was born a McLaggan in Stillwater. Many of the stories I heard about the McLaggans were from my grandmother. However, not until I researched their lives and the stories I heard throughout my life did I feel the closeness with this family that were a few generations apart from me. Beloved family stories, church and census records, directories, newspaper articles, publications, and obituaries brought me even closer to the ancestors I heard the most about and came so close to knowing.

McLaggan or MacLaggan?

The McLaggans were a strong, proud, and hardworking Scottish family with high moral values and integrity. In the 1700s, the McLaggan ancestors migrated from Scotland to New Brunswick, Canada, then to Stillwater around 1867.

A frequent topic of conversation among family is: "Is it McLaggan or MacLaggan?" This lowercase letter *a*, at the beginning of their surname, has created a bit of a debate and mystery over the last several generations. While researching many McLaggan generations from Scotland to New Brunswick, the beginning of their surname was most often written as *Mac* during the 1700s in Scotland. While in Canada for many years, *Mc* was the chosen way the family would write their name. Once in Stillwater, the beginning of their last name remained constant written as *Mc*, until the twentieth century. In the early 1900s, the spelling was never consistent, sometimes *Mc* sometimes *Mac*. During a bit more research on the *Mc* vs. *Mac* controversy, I found that even in Scotland, *Mc* and *Mac* basically mean the same thing. It is also said that *Mc* is the abbreviated form of *Mac*.

Therefore, within the pages of this book, you will see it spelled both ways, depending on what source it was taken from.

It's now time to discover more about who these Scottish McLaggans were.

The Scottish Family from New Brunswick

The McLaggan family who migrated to Stillwater had Highlander ancestry from Scotland. Their ancestors were a self-sufficient group of immigrants who were industrious with unceasing energy. When the McLaggan family left Scotland and arrived in New Brunswick, they cultivated their land and used hand mills to grind their grain. They built log houses and barns, and dug long and deep trenches, called saw pits, for the ease of cutting timber. The depth of a saw pit was approximately six feet, and the length was fourteen to fifteen feet long. When they were ready to begin sawing, the men would position and secure the timber over the pit length-wise. One man stood on the log above the saw pit, and another man stood below inside the pit. A long and rigid whipsaw, with a handle at each end, was used to cut the length of the log. Beginning at one end of the log, the men sawed through it, then up and down the length of the log, to create long wooden planks.[38] In addition to this exhausting undertaking, they hollowed out large tree trunks to make canoes for journeys on the river when the roads were impossible to travel. They made honey and tapped maple trees for syrup, and grew flax that they processed into linen, making sure to use all that was produced. If they wore clothing made from cotton, it was reserved for Sunday church services.[39]

Kenneth William McLaggan and his wife, Rebecca (McRae), both born in New Brunswick, arrived in Stillwater, Minnesota around 1867, along with their oldest son, John Alexander McLaggan, also born in New Brunswick in 1865.

When the McLaggan family arrived in Stillwater, John Alexander would have been about two years old. Rebecca gave birth to three more children in Stillwater: Kenneth, Jr., in 1868, Eva Rebecca, in 1871, and Roderick, in 1874.

The home they resided in for many years was located at 206 South

Owens Street. However, before they moved to the Owens Street home, they also lived in other places, including 1007 West Ramsey Street.

Lumberman, Teamster, and Contractor

For the first twenty years in Stillwater, the patriarch of the family, Kenneth McLaggan, Sr., was in the logging business. He was employed upon his own responsibility, which in today's terms would mean self-employed. He has been described as a robust individual, the essence of a lumberman. For many years he logged on the St. Croix as a teamster, handling and driving a team of horses, pulling a bobsled full of freshly cut timber that glided above the snow.

The lumbermen would engage in their trade during the winter months, when there was a large quantity of snow and ice present upon the ground, which made it easy to transport lumber on large bobsleds. During the cold and wintry season, having the gliding blades on the bobsleds working in unison with the team of horses would make transporting the heavy logs more efficient, and a less difficult task for the animal laborers.

The men worked diligently in the woods during the winter months before the spring thaw, when they would begin work in the sawmill. After the trees were cut, they stacked the enormous logs high on top of each other upon the long bobsled in an orderly fashion. When the sled was loaded and wasn't able to handle any more timber, the teamster would begin to call out his commands to the team of horses ahead of him to begin to pull the heavy load forward on the icy path. The teamster would no doubt be praying for a safe journey on his way to deliver the massive load of timber, as the job of teamster and lumberjack was a very dangerous career during the logging era. There were many accidents and casualties that went along with that chosen career, some quite horrific.

After several years of working as a teamster, Kenneth McLaggan discontinued that profession and became a contractor, grading streets for the City of Stillwater. He would hire laborers for the project to create a level base or appropriate slope for an intended street. One contract he obtained was for the grading of Olive Street.

IN THE NEWS

The Stillwater Messenger, October 4, 1890

The contract for grading Olive Street from Second to Main was on Monday let to Kenneth McLaggan at a cost of $525. Mr. McLaggan has already placed a large number of men and teams at work, and the street will soon be finished.

After his careers of logging on the St. Croix as a teamster and grading streets throughout the town, Kenneth McLaggan, Sr., would later become employed by the Musser and Sauntry Lumber Company, where he was hired as foreman. As foreman, he would find the best location to set up camp for the lumbermen for the duration of their time there. His responsibilities would also include the purchase of horses, logging equipment, and camping supplies for the lumbermen, who would make the new logging camp their temporary home away from home.

John Alexander McLaggan

The oldest son of Kenneth and Rebecca McLaggan was John Alexander McLaggan, my future great-grandfather.

John received a good education in the Stillwater school district that served him well throughout his life. Like his father, he seemed to also have a good work ethic, although John's future career was definitely not as laborious as his father's.

After being educated in the Stillwater school district, several clothing companies employed John. He began as a clerk, then a bookkeeper, and lastly a traveling salesman, for different clothing companies.

While searching for John on the "hints" on an ancestry website, one hint came up in a directory from St. Louis, Missouri when he was twenty years old. In the 1885 St. Louis Directory, there appeared a John McLaggan. He is listed as working for a gentleman's clothing company. It is very possible that he moved to St. Louis for a short time, where he landed a job working for a clothing company, and "learned the ropes," which led to a career in that particular industry. The company listed in the St. Louis directory is Crawford and Co. Clothing, a dealer in gentlemen furnishings and goods, clothing, and accessories.

Beginning in 1890 and all the subsequent years, John is listed in Stillwater directories as working for a variety of clothing companies and stores in Stillwater. Throughout his life in Stillwater, he worked for such stores as: Voigt and Scott, The Standard Clothing Co., Brodeen and Mattson, and Kolliner Brothers and Newman, as a traveling salesman.

Perhaps his handsome looks and friendly demeanor helped him land his positions at clothing companies that would no doubt need an intelligent and attractive gentleman representing their up-and-coming clothing lines to prospective clientele. John McLaggan has also been described as being a very kind and approachable man. Whatever the reason for him beginning a career in the clothing industry, it served him well, as the descendants of the family have always been told, that he and his family were always "dressed to the nines."

John Alexander McLaggan, circa 1890
Photograph Courtesy of Florence Jane Wennerberg

Other McLaggan Children

Kenneth and Rebecca's other children after John Alexander were all born in Stillwater. Their first child born in Stillwater was Kenneth, Jr., born in 1868, who married Nellie Sinnott in 1897. The two moved to Gordon, Wisconsin, and had five children; Evelyn, Will, John, Roderick, and Walter.

The only daughter of Kenneth, Sr., and Rebecca, was Eva Rebecca, born in 1871. She was a school teacher and principal for the Stillwater School District for many years. Eva taught at the District 16 School beginning around 1890 or 1891, and would later become the principal at the new Nelson School beginning in 1897, the same year it opened for the Stillwater youth.

Kenneth and Rebecca's youngest son, Roderick, born in 1874, would eventually move to Spokane, Washington, where he met and married Margaret Mahanna. He would live there for the rest of his life.

The Wrights and McLaggans Unite

During the time that John McLaggan, son of Kenneth and Rebecca McLaggan, met his future wife, Ivy Wright, daughter of Addison Wright and Anna Maria Tobin, John was employed as a clerk at Voigt and Scott Clothing Company, located at 237 South Main Street.

Since John had a presence on Main Street in Stillwater, arriving and departing the clothing store on a daily basis, perhaps Ivy caught his eye when she went out

John Alexander McLaggan,
circa 1894
Photograph Courtesy of
Florence Jane Wennerberg

shopping with friends or her father, as he exited the clothing store in his fine gentleman's suit and bowler hat.

Ivy Maria Wright, circa 1894
Photograph Courtesy of
Mary Kirst

As their homes were only blocks away from each other, they may have met through mutual acquaintances or John's younger siblings. John was eight years older than Ivy, and his sister, Eva, and brother, Roderick, were closer in age to his soon-to-be wife.

Ivy Wright and John McLaggan were married at St. Michael's Catholic Church on Tuesday, September 11, 1894. Their marriage was officiated by Father Charles Corcoran, and their witnesses were J.R. McGarry and Mary M. McDougal

The home where Ivy and John would reside for several years after their marriage was located at 417 South Harriett Street. This is the home where they began their family, welcoming into the world the first four of their five daughters.

John McLaggan and Ivy Wright, circa 1894
Photograph Courtesy of Mary Kirst
and Florence Jane Wennerberg

PART TWO

CHAPTER ELEVEN

The "Little Women" of Stillwater

Little Women, the book by Louisa May Alcott (and the many successfully recreated movies portraying it), has always reminded me of stories I heard from my grandmother Mildred about her and her sisters' lives. She and her sisters were all born and raised in Stillwater in the 1890s through the early 1900s.

Written in the year 1868, *Little Women* tells an endearing story of the lives of four sisters living in Concord, Massachusetts, and growing up during the mid-nineteenth century, during the Civil War era. The year the book was written and what it depicted was earlier than the lives of my grandmother and her sisters; however, it includes stories here and there that are reminiscent of the stories my grandmother told me. The triumphs and struggles she and her sisters endured throughout the years that can be compared with Alcott's famous book make me realize that history really does repeat itself.

Mildred Maria

After their marriage vows, John and Ivy McLaggan began their family without delay. The couple's first daughter, Mildred McLaggan, my maternal Grandmother, was born on November 1, 1894. Mildred was always told by her parents that she weighed only one pound when she was born. They told her they placed her in a cigar box near the wood-burning stove to keep her warm and to assist in her development. She obviously thrived with a cigar box and stove as a make-shift incubator, as she lived to be almost eighty years old.

John McLaggan was known to be a very agreeable and amiable

gentleman, a gentle man in every sense of the word. Although he was Presbyterian, he agreed to have their daughter and future children baptized at St. Michael's Catholic Church, as he knew his wife was raised Catholic and was also baptized at St. Michael's twenty-two years earlier, it being her family's parish since the 1850s.

At the age of six months, Mildred was baptized as "Maria Mildred" by Father Charles Corcoran, on May 5, 1895, at St. Michael's Catholic Church in Stillwater. Her godparents were her mother's brother and his wife, Addison Wright, Jr., and Mary Wright.

Mildred McLaggan, circa 1895
Photograph Courtesy of Mary Kirst
and Florence Jane Wennerberg

Marguerite

One year after Mildred's birth, John and Ivy welcomed their second daughter, Marguerite, born in October 1895.

Mildred was delighted with her first little playmate who was added to the McLaggan family when Mildred was just one year old. In future years, when Mildred would speak of her sister, one could tell she had a great fondness for Marguerite, and a noticeably broken heart.

Marguerite was baptized by Father Patrick Kissane as "Eva Marguerite" at St. Michael's Catholic Church on May 31, 1896, at the age of seven months. Her godparents were Samuel and Maria Matthews.

Marguerite and Mildred McLaggan,
circa 1896
Photograph Courtesy of Mary Kirst
and Florence Jane Wennerberg

The two little sisters would only have one year to spend together. They knew each other only as toddlers, as Marguerite suddenly died one year after her birth, in October 1896.

Mildred's great fondness for her little sister, and the memories she held in her heart, may have had more to do with the cherished photograph of the two of them, than the memories she actually possessed, as she herself was almost two years old the day her baby sister passed to her heavenly home.

Even though Mildred was quite young at the time, she always relayed her memories of that day quite vividly. The day Marguerite died, Mildred remembered standing near her mother, watching her sobbing uncontrollably while holding the baby. The baby was motionless, lying in her mother's arms. Ivy clung tightly to Marguerite, refusing to believe the reality of that moment in time.

The brokenness experienced by her young mother could have also contributed to the memories Mildred carried with her throughout her life, as the clearest memory she always spoke of regarding that day was how her mother had to be coaxed to release her powerful grip when giving up her lifeless little child.

IN THE NEWS

The Stillwater Messenger, October, 31, 1896

The funeral of Ivy Marguerite, the little daughter of Mr. and Mrs. John McLaggan, was held from the family residence on Sunday after noon.

After the death of a beloved family member, no matter what age, it's difficult for the remaining members to move forward and come to grips with the permanency of that individual not being present any longer, to realize the truth of the bittersweet phrase "life goes on." A phrase I never cared for, really, due to the reality of its somewhat ill-mannered and blunt message. But, life does go on, and soon the McLaggans realized they had to move forward and return to a normal life, especially for their daughter, Mildred.

Mildred McLaggan, circa, 1896
Photograph Courtesy of Mary Kirst
and Florence Jane Wennerberg

Almost one year after the death of Marguerite, John McLaggan's sister, Eva McLaggan, was hired for the position of Principal of the new Nelson

School, which was completed in September 1897.[40]

IN THE NEWS

The Stillwater Messenger, September 18, 1897

Prof. Weld assigned Miss Eva McLaggan as principal of the new Nelson School, Miss Lulu Meeds of the new Lincoln Building, and Miss O'Donnell as instructor of mathematics in the high school and asked the board to pass upon his action, which they did, making the assignments permanent.

Florence Rebecca

The third daughter born to John and Ivy McLaggan was welcomed with great excitement in 1898. Mildred, at the age of four, was thrilled about the arrival of her new little sister. There's a bit of a mystery surrounding Florence's baptism, as her baptism record shows she was baptized privately, and then again three months later. Florence was baptized at a younger age compared to the two previous McLaggan girls, who were six and seven months old, respectively. She was baptized as "Florence Rebecca" on February 19, 1898 at six weeks old, in church records written in Latin as *privatus*, meaning private. Included in the same church record for Florence there is another baptism date of May 20, 1898, stated in Latin as *caeremonia*, meaning holy ceremony or sacred rite. The baptizing priest is listed as Father Charles Corcoran; however, only one godparent is listed on the baptismal record, Anna Kelley.

Perhaps Ivy didn't want to wait too long to have her third daughter baptized, as their second daughter, Marguerite, died at one year old. If Florence became ill after she was born, Ivy may have baptized her infant herself, fearing the same fate as Marguerite.

According to the Baltimore Catechism from the Catholic Church, first published in 1885, the *Code of Canon Law*, Chapter III, Section 867, states: "An infant in danger of death is to be baptized without delay." There should also be at least one person present to witness the private baptism.

Mildred and Florence McLaggan, circa 1900 Photograph Courtesy of Florence Jane Wennberberg

An infant that is baptized privately should then be brought to the church for the priest to complete the formal Rite of Baptism. He then enters the private baptism date as the official date in church records; the latter date would be the date the sacred ceremonial ritual was performed. Perhaps Ivy baptized her daughter Florence herself, having her friend Anna Kelley present during the private baptism of her six-week-old infant, and therefore only one godparent could be listed on the church's official baptism record. Since Florence received a private baptism date as well as an additional ceremony date at St. Michael's Catholic Church, this is a very likely scenario of what occurred.

Dorothea Ann

One year after Florence's birth, Ivy gave birth to another daughter in February 1899. She was baptized as Dorothea Ann on April 23, 1899, at the age of two months. Her godparents were Francis Kelley and Maria McDougal; the baptizing priest was Father Charles Corcoran.

John McLaggan had worked for several clothing companies for many years and was advancing in his career during the time his and Ivy's daughters were born. Sometime shortly after Dorothea Ann was born, who began to go by the name of Dorothy, the family of five—John, Ivy and their three daughters—moved to 611 West Churchhill Street.

While living on Churchhill Street, John went from clerk to bookkeeper at Brodeen and Mattson. After working for Brodeen and Mattson for many years, he changed companies and began working for Kolliner Bros and Newman as a traveling sales agent, where he worked until his retirement many years later.

Eva McLaggan, The Adoring Aunt

*E*va McLaggan, the sister to the McLaggan girls' father, John, is remembered as a very kind and thoughtful woman. She was a devoted teacher and principal at local Stillwater schools; however, she was first a devoted and adoring aunt.

Before Aunt Eva married, she took the pleasure of spoiling her nieces, as she had no children of her own at the time. She took them to visit with friends, or to go "out on the town" to shop on Main Street, for whatever her little nieces desired. They would occasionally attire themselves in special fitting outfits or dress up "fancy" for special photography sessions at local photography studios on Main Street.

Aunt Eva Rebecca McLaggan with niece Mildred McLaggan, circa 1899
Photograph Courtesy of Mary Kirst and Florence Jane Wennerberg

IN THE NEWS

The Stillwater Messenger, August 8, 1903,

The marriage of Dr. Ernest E. Wells and Miss Eva R. MacLaggan occurred Wednesday afternoon at the residence of S.J. Kennedy. Both are favorably known in the city and will have the congratulations of many friends. They will make Stillwater their home.

Eva Rebecca McLaggan, circa 1903
Photograph Courtesy of Roberta
Feyereisen, granddaughter of
Dr. and Mrs. E.E. Wells

Dr. Ernest E. Wells, circa 1903
Photograph Courtesy of Roberta
Feyereisen, granddaughter of
Dr. and Mrs. E.E. Wells

Dr. and Mrs. Eva McLaggan Wells went on to have two daughters, Adele and Janet.

House Calls in the Early 1900s

*S*ome might say it's a blessing to have a doctor in the family, others might disagree.

Mildred, who in later years was a woman of few words, would relay this particular cringeworthy story to my family and me when we would ask her to tell us a story from her childhood. As she began to tell us this story from her youth, we would all go wide-eyed while listening, but we never tired of hearing it. I'm sure it was an experience our grandmother could never forget, even if she wanted to.

ildred's Aunt Eva was married to Dr. Wells, so immediate house calls in the early 1900s from the doctor were not a problem for the McLaggan family.

When Mildred was a young girl, she became quite ill, and her parents were in fear of a dreadful outcome. Dr. Wells examined the young McLaggan daughter and diagnosed Mildred with tonsillitis, which usually is accompanied by a high fever, a sore throat, difficulty swallowing, etc. Her tonsils were extremely red and swollen and needed to be taken out, due to them becoming infected, and a turn for the worse could be close at hand.

Dr. Wells advised Ivy and John that Mildred had to have her tonsils removed without delay. He used the kitchen table for a makeshift operating table and proceeded with the operation on young Mildred, apparently without anesthetic. Mildred had her tonsils taken out promptly, surrounded by her family and lying upon the family's furniture used for daily meals. No wonder she never forgot that event, which I would classify as traumatic for anyone, no matter what age.

What seems like an archaic medical emergency operation in the current day was a somewhat normal event in the early 1900s, including the use of a kitchen table for surgery.

Cousins

esides, siblings, the next best thing for a family's enrichment and lessons in getting along with others is their relationships with cousins. Cousins are usually the first set of friends children have. The McLaggan girls, Mildred, Florence, and Dorothy, were very close to their cousins, the five children of their father's brother, their uncle Kenneth McLaggan, Jr., and his wife, their aunt Nellie (Sinnott).

A year or two after Uncle Kenneth and Aunt Nellie were married, the two moved to Gordon, Wisconsin, where all their children were born: Evelyn, Will, John, Roderick, and Walter. Even though they didn't live in Stillwater, the McLaggan cousins would get together quite often and enjoyed being in each other's company, either in Stillwater or Gordon. Mildred was very close to her cousin Evelyn, as well as with her cousin Will, as she would often state, "Next to Evelyn, Will was my favorite." Will could be quite the instigator from time to time, due to his shenanigans.

McLaggan Cousins. Front row; Florence, Cousin Evelyn, back row, Cousin Will, Dorothy and Mildred. Photograph Courtesy of Mary Kirst and Florence Jane Wennerberg

On hot and humid Minnesota summer days in the early 1900s, Mildred, her sisters, and cousin Evelyn would often go swimming in nearby lakes when they visited each other in either Gordon or Stillwater.

On a particular hot summer day in the early 1900s, after the girls enjoyed themselves cooling off in a refreshing lake, they exited the water wearing only their water-drenched undergarments—camisoles and knee-length, lace-trimmed drawers—and couldn't find where they had laid their clothes. They thought they remembered what part of the shore they had set them down on, but were unable to locate them after combing the shores of the lake. Suddenly, they heard the giggles and laughs of Evelyn's brother, Will, and his friend, and spotted them cackling behind a nearby tree, holding the clothes hostage.

Mildred was feeling quite embarrassed that day; however, she forgave Will. This "unspeakable" prank didn't keep him out of Mildred's favor as she continued to state many times that "next to Evelyn, Will was my favorite."

Front row; Florence, Dorothy;
back row; cousin Evelyn and Mildred.
Photograph courtesy of Florence Jane Wennerberg

Moving in with Grandfather Addison

After John and Ivy and their three daughters left their Churchhill Street home sometime around 1905, they moved in with Ivy's father, Addison Wright, at his home at 518 West Olive Street. At that time, their daughters, Mildred, Florence, and Dorothy, would have been approximately eleven, seven, and six years old, respectively.

Perhaps it had something to do with her grandfather Addison Wright and her uncle, Addison, Jr. (fondly known as Uncle Addy), being musically inclined and part-time musicians in Stillwater, that Mildred became an accomplished pianist.

Addison and Uncle Addy would bring music into the home when the two of them would entertain Mildred and her family on Olive Street. Their home was always filled with music, song, and dance. She and her sisters were a receptive audience to the in-home concerts. Grandfather Addison relayed that in the "early days," he would play his fiddle for special balls, town dances, and informal barn dances in Stillwater.

Mildred's father surprised her one day and presented her with a piano. Soon after her lessons commenced, she went above and beyond what was expected, as she picked up the talent of "playing by ear" for just about anything someone would ask her to play. They just had to hum a few bars if she didn't already know the tune and she began to play it with ease.

Left to right: Florence, Dorothy and Mildred McLaggan, Photograph Courtesy of Florence Jane Wennerberg

IN THE NEWS

The Stillwater Messenger, August 18, 1906

Addison Wright, Sr., is home from several months' residence at Winton, Minn. If the fish stories are true that Addison tells about, we should judge he would hate to leave that neck of the woods.

A Home of Their Own

For many years, John and Ivy rented the homes they lived in while raising their daughters. Sometime between 1910 and 1912, John was doing well enough as a traveling sales agent for the Kolliner Bros company to be able to purchase a home for his family on Pine Street. The McLaggan daughters would have been approximately the following ages: Mildred, fifteen, Florence, eleven, and Dorothy, ten, when they moved a couple of blocks away from where they were previously living, at Grandfather Addison's home on Olive Street, to their new home at 703 West Pine Street.

IN THE NEWS

The World, Evening Edition, New York, N.Y, April 15, 1912

LINERS TAKE OFF PASSENGERS: TITANIC REPORTED SINKING

Gigantic Bow of the Titanic Crumpled by Collision with Iceberg.

World's Biggest Ship Reported in Bad Shape After Collision at Night and Now Being Towed to Halifax by the Allen Liner Virginian.

SAY PASSENGERS WERE TAKEN OFF

An Associated Press despatch from London read: "All passengers of the Titanic were taken off safely at 3.30 o'clock, according to a wireless message, to Halifax, Nova Scotia, relayed by a news agency here."

New York Tribune, April 16, 1912

1,340 PERISH AS TITANIC SINKS; ONLY 886, MOSTLY WOMEN AND CHILDREN RESCUED

Jeanette Adalaide

My Stillwater rendition of *Little Women* wouldn't be complete without adding one more McLaggan daughter for John and Ivy.

Surprise! It's another girl! The youngest of the McLaggan girls, Jeanette, affectionately known as Jean, was born to Ivy and John McLaggan on August 30, 1913, which just so happened to be her father's birthday. She was fourteen years younger than Dorothy, the previous daughter born to them, fifteen years younger than Florence, and almost nineteen years younger than Mildred.

The eldest of the sisters, Mildred, was a bit shocked when her parents announced they were having another baby at their ages of forty and forty-eight, as she and her other two sisters were almost fully-grown young women at the time of the blessed announcement. It's a funny thing to think that Mildred could have ever felt shocked or even embarrassed about her parents having another baby at their ages, as Mildred and Jean became very close over the years, even being so many years apart.

Ivy Wright-McLaggan and daughter, Jean, circa 1913 Photograph Courtesy of Jon Meister

At five weeks old, Jean was baptized by Father Charles Corcoran as "Jeanette Adelaide," on October 5, 1913, at St. Michael's Catholic Church. Jean's godparents were her mother's brother, Addison Wright, Jr., and Stella Matthews.

At the time of Jean's birth in 1913, all of the McLaggan girls were unmarried and still living at home with their parents. The three oldest were thrilled as they welcomed their new baby sister. Her sisters enjoyed taking Jean out and about with them in Stillwater, just to show her off. I believe she may have been a bit spoiled by her big sisters, in a good way, and I'm sure it was a much-needed break for their mother, Ivy.

Jean McLaggan, circa 1915
Photograph Courtesy of
Jon Meister

Jean McLaggan, circa 1916
Photograph Courtesy of
Jon Meister

IN THE NEWS

The Minneapolis Morning Tribune, November 10, 1915

STILLWATER

Dr. E.E. Wells, the coroner, assumed the duties of sheriff on the death of Sheriff L. D. Jarehow. Yesterday he appointed Ezra J. Spindle to continue as deputy sheriff.

Dr. Ernest E. Wells
Photograph Courtesy of
Roberta Feyereisen

Dr. E.E. Wells, the husband to Eva (McLaggan) Wells, held the temporary position as sheriff for two days in 1915, on November 10th and 11th, until the new sheriff was elected.

IN THE NEWS

The New York Times, May 30, 1916

J. J. Hill Dead In St. Paul Home At The Age of 77

Special to THE NEW YORK TIMES

ST. PAUL, May 29—James J. Hill, builder of the "Northwest Empire," died at 9:30 A.M. today at his house, 240 Summit Avenue.

In his room, in the southeast corner on the second floor of the brownstone house overlooking the city to which he came sixty years ago as a clerk, the end came.

The active pallbearers will be M. R. Brown, private secretary to J. J. Hill; Ralph Budd, assistant to the President, Great Northern Railway Company; C. W. Gordon, President Gordon and Ferguson Co.; J. M. Gruber, Vice President Great Northern Railway Company; W. P. Kenny, Vice President Great Northern Railway Company; Theodore Schulze, President Foot, Schulze and Co.; P. L. Howe, Minneapolis; G. A. MacPherson, intimate friend of the Hill family; J. J. Toomey, official of the Great Northern Railway and the First National Bank, and Charles Maitland, for twenty-five years a coachman in the Hill family.

A Modest, Honest, Upright Citizen

Addison Wright, Sr., witnessed many of the changes and improvements in the thriving little town of Stillwater from the middle to the end of the nineteenth century, and more advances as he welcomed in the twentieth century in 1900.

When Addison died in March 1919, there were obituaries in several Minnesota newspapers from Winton to Stillwater, announcing the death of the well-respected man from Stillwater. Not as many announcements as when James J. Hill died three years earlier, but enough for his family, friends, and acquaintances to remember him as an honest, upright citizen.

I have developed a great deal of fondness and admiration while researching Addison Wright. He raised five children, often by himself, beginning in 1875, and carried on through the daily toils that life had thrown at him, which on many occasions would seem unimaginable to many. Being a single father for many years I'm sure was quite challenging, but one he obviously took on without hesitation. The closeness I believe he had with his children cannot be understated.

This well-respected man who was proud to say he was born in Durham, New York, always told others where he came from, a heritage he liked to share with his children and grandchildren.

Throughout my research, it wasn't very often that I came across an error in Addison's records stating that he was from some place other than New York. This was even evident on his death certificate. The certificate showed his daughter-in-law as the informant, and even the details regarding his place of birth as the little town of Durham, New York are correct.

As I mourn Addison's life on the next few pages, I wonder if perhaps the saying of remembering who you are and remembering where you came from may have originated from him or his mother, as that seemed to be a constant theme of their official records. It wouldn't surprise me if it came from Addison, as he was the type of father who would instill a certain esteem within his children and would want them to remember their beginnings.

IN THE NEWS

The Stillwater Gazette, Wednesday, March 12, 1919

DIED AT WINTON.

Addison Wright, Sr. Called to His Final Rest Tuesday Old Time Resident.

Addison Wright, Sr. aged nearly 78 years of age died at Winton, Minn. of cancer, Tuesday March 12, 1919, after an illness of many months . . .

Mr. Wright went to Winton about ten or twelve years ago where he made his home with his son, Addison, Jr. Deceased came to Stillwater in company with the late Prof. J.L. Jones more than fifty years ago, making this his home until he removed to Winton. He was a painter by trade. He served during the civil war as a musician and was connected with the band and orchestra organization in Stillwater for many years.

Mr. Wright was a modest, honest upright citizen who leaves a large circle of friends who will extend the warmest sympathy to the bereaved ones left to mourn...

Surviving are the sons, Addison Jr. and Cleveland George Wright living at Winton, and Mrs. J.A. McLaggan and Mrs. Bert Daily of this city and Mrs. W. J. Harper, a sister.

Addison's Legacy

The selling of Addison's house after his death would be the first time in forty-eight years that someone other than Addison Wright owned the family home he had built for himself and his first wife, Anna Maria Tobin, in 1871, at 518 West Olive Street.

His house on Olive Street, in the Webster's Addition, was listed as being appraised at $1200 in his probate record in April 1919. In addition to Addison, Sr., living there for so many years with his family, his daughter Ivy also lived there for numerous years at different times throughout her life. The Olive Street home was where she was born and grew to adulthood with all her siblings. Then, several years after her marriage to John McLaggan, Ivy and John moved in with her father at the Olive Street home, along with three of their daughters, Mildred, Florence, and Dorothy, to reside for several years. I'm sure the sale of the Olive Street home evoked some bittersweet memories for Ivy, who shared and witnessed so much of her father's life experiences there.

A statement from Addison's daughter, Ivy (Wright) McLaggan, included in his Probate record states:

Ivy MacLaggan being duly sworn, on oath says that she is a daughter of the deceased; that for many years he made his home with affiant and in her family, except at certain times when he would be visiting his son, Addison Wright at Winton, Minnesota, that he always made Stillwater his home, and would not consent to reside elsewhere, that she is familiar with his affairs.

Addison was laid to rest in Fairview Cemetery in Stillwater, Minnesota on March 14, 1919, next to his mother, Mary Ann (Wright) Jones, and her second husband, Joseph L. Jones, in one of the three plots his mother purchased in 1894.

CHAPTER TWELVE

The "Little Women" of Stillwater and St. Paul

The daughters of Ivy (Wright) and John McLaggan became very strong and independent women. The four daughters who lived into adulthood had no brothers. This didn't stop John McLaggan, being a father to only daughters, from instilling in his children a sense of independence, and the love of fishing, nature, and the outdoors, which continues today among some of the descendants.

Mildred Trains to Become a Nurse

The memorable and cringeworthy surgery the oldest daughter, Mildred, endured in having her tonsils removed many years earlier by her uncle, Dr. Ernest Wells, obviously didn't have too much of a traumatic impact on her, as she decided to become involved in the nursing profession years later. When Mildred was in her early twenties, around 1914, she began to train as a nurse under the direction of Dr. Wells.

After several years of training by his side, Mildred became employed as a nurse, working for a private family in St. Paul as a result of the connections and acquaintances Dr. Wells had in the city. On her workdays, Mildred would take the streetcar from Stillwater to St. Paul and back again, which may be one of the reasons she became to be a strong and independent woman.

The Flu Pandemic

Influenza—a single word from 1918 to 1920 that would make anyone gasp for fear of death. This was not a discriminating disease by any means. It was not selective toward any of its victims throughout the world, or the little town of Stillwater.

John and Ivy's daughter, Florence, seemed to have always been a delicate young girl from the time she was born. It was Florence that had a private baptism at St. Michael's Church, as well as an additional baptismal ceremony shortly after her birth, which still remains shrouded in mystery.

Florence was just twenty-one when she contracted the uninvited illness, also known as the Spanish Flu, during its peak in 1919.[41] Her parents and sisters were terrified that their dear Florence would become one of the many victims of this loathsome disease that would intrude upon anyone without advance notice. The youngest daughter, Jean, was only six years old at the time of her sister's illness, which was an added fear and concern for her parents and sisters.

When the pandemic subsided in the winter of 1920, at least 50 million people died worldwide, including over 500,000 in the United States.

IN THE NEWS

The Washington Times, September 21, 1918

INFLUENZA CLAIMS VICTIM IN CAPTIAL.

Outbreak of "Spanish" influenza among Washington civilian population was revealed today when the first fatal case had been reported to the District Health Office. . .

PLAGUE IN CHICAGO, September 21—Spanish influenza has invaded Chicago, and army training students, at Lewis Institute in consequence, are now under quarantine...

El Paso Herald, September 27, 1918

INFLUENZA WILL SPREAD WEST, IS BELIEF,
MALDAY SWEEPING ALL OF 13 CAMPS, CAUSES MANY MORE DEATHS.
SITUATION IS VERY SERIOUS

Tragedies of all kinds were presented on the world stage, including irreversible damage to those who did survive. Florence was one of the fortunate ones who survived the influenza pandemic; however, she continued to suffer with frequent illnesses due to the weakening of her immune system. Her sister, Mildred, who was trained as a nurse, wanted to make sure Florence would have the best care to get her back to health, and would often take her sister to doctor appointments and be there for her whenever possible.

Florence never worked or had any type of career, as she was sickly during her "recovery." She always lived at home with her parents and did what she could to help her mother with the household chores and to help care for her little sister, Jean.

Mildred's Life Is About to Change

Mildred's uncle, Dr. Wells, had many colleagues in St. Paul. There was a particular pharmacist or druggist, as they were called, located at a store in St. Paul at Third and Maria (Ma-RYE-ah). Dr. Wells would have his niece bring in prescriptions to the Third Street pharmacy for the druggist to fill for his St. Paul patients. The druggist became well acquainted with Mildred due to her frequent visits to the drug store. He enjoyed conversing with her and thought she was a lovely young woman. During subsequent conversations with Dr. Wells, the St. Paul druggist told him that he knew of a very nice and successful gentleman that lived nearby in St. Paul, who would frequent the store to purchase cigars. The druggist thought that the gentleman and Mildred should meet, as he believed they would hit it off. The druggist and Dr. Wells decided to be matchmakers for these two unsuspecting individuals.

On a particular day, shortly after discussing matchmaking plans for the two, Dr. Wells phoned the druggist to tell him that Mildred was on her way with a new prescription to be filled; that put the wheels in motion. The druggist called the gentleman from St. Paul, who lived just a half block away on Maria, and asked him to come into the store. Mildred met the gentleman that day, and they were quite smitten with each other.

The man Mildred McLaggan met that day, and would later marry, was Francis Frederick Brown, better known as Fred F. Brown. He was born in Dubuque, Iowa, in 1881, to parents of Irish descent, who both migrated from Ireland when they were young. His family moved to St. Paul when Fred was a child. He did very well in the St. Paul school district and continued his education to study law at the St. Paul College of Law.

On November 3, 1914, he was elected to the Minnesota House of Representatives for Ramsey County and served until January 1, 1917.[42] At the time of his election, he was engaged at Cook Construction Company, and would later become employed by the Great Northern Railway Company.

Fred's brother, Martin R. Brown, was also employed by the Great Northern Railway as the private secretary to James J. Hill, the founder and chairman for the Great Northern Railway, for the last thirteen years of the "Empire Builder's" life.[43]

As Fred also studied law, he would occasionally do some work on the side for James J. Hill, along with his brother Martin. They would be invited to dine now and again with the Hills in their Summit Avenue mansion, in St. Paul. These events occurred before Fred married Mildred McLaggan from Stillwater, as James J. Hill died in 1916. Fred's brother, also known as, M. R. Brown, was an honored colleague and served as a pallbearer at James J. Hill's funeral.[44]

A Pre-Valentine Day Wedding

*I*t was a Wednesday morning at nine o'clock, February 11, 1920, when Mildred and Fred were united in marriage at St. Michael's Catholic Church. The officiant was Father Charles Corcoran, the same priest who officiated at Mildred's parents' wedding, twenty-six years earlier, as well as the priest who had baptized Mildred at six months old.

Mildred's sister, Florence, had recovered enough after contracting influenza one year earlier to have the honor of being her attendant on her special day. Norbert Reilly of St. Paul stood by the side of his cousin Fred, as his honored attendant.

On the day of their wedding, a detailed announcement regarding the happy occasion appeared in the later edition of the *Stillwater Gazette*.

Mildred McLaggan
Photograph Courtesy
of Mary Kirst

Fred F. Brown
Photograph Courtesy
of Mary Kirst

IN THE NEWS

The Stillwater Gazette, February 11, 1920

McLaggan-Brown

A very pretty wedding took place this morning at St. Michael's church when Miss Mildred McLaggan, daughter of Mr. and Mrs. J.A. McLaggan, 703 Pine street, became the bride of Frederick F. Brown of St. Paul . . .

The article continues to describe the ceremony and celebration. It gives details of what the bride was wearing: "a navy-blue suit with hat to match." Her ensemble was finished with a corsage bouquet of bride's roses. The fashion was becoming more modern during that era, and a woman's attire called a "suit" was indeed more modern, but still feminine and quite fashionable.

For 1920s fashion, I imagine her suit being just about ankle length and made of high-quality material, as her father was a dedicated individual in the clothing industry, well-versed in the fine quality of an assortment of fabrics. To finish off her suit, Mildred's matching jacket would have been fitted at the waist, with its length ending slightly at or below the hips.

Her sister, Florence, wore a blue taffeta gown with a corsage bouquet of Ophelia roses. As Florence stood beside Mildred on the day of her sister's wedding, I have to imagine it was an honor that she took quite seriously, full of love and excitement with overwhelming emotions as her close sister and friend was now marrying and moving out of the family home, many miles away to St. Paul.

I'm also quite sure Florence wasn't the only one feeling honored to be standing beside her sister that day. I have no doubt that Mildred was not only feeling blessed at having Florence present, but also relieved, as she saw firsthand how Florence fought a battle with the unrelenting illness that tried to take her away from the family.

At the conclusion of the wedding ceremony, the bridal party, along with family and close friends, traveled a few blocks away from the church to the home of the McLaggans at 703 West Pine Street, where a special wedding breakfast was served. For an added touch to the wedding breakfast celebration, their home was fully adorned with Valentine decorations, as Valentine's Day was just a few days away.

Mildred was known as a very practical woman, so it comes as no surprise that she wore a suit for her wedding ceremony that day. She and her new husband would be traveling by train for their honeymoon, and her suit was more functional for travel. Perhaps while preparing for the special day, she decided to choose an outfit she could remain in for the ceremony and events of the day, as well as the evening's long journey ahead to Chicago.

Traveling by train was very common for their family in future years, at little or no cost, as Fred became a traveling contracting freight agent, similar to a broker, for the Great Northern Railway.

Mildred was the first and only McLaggan daughter to leave Stillwater to begin the family's legacy in St. Paul.

ildred had no problem adjusting to the lifestyle of a St. Paul "city woman." There wasn't a challenge she couldn't take on. Reviewing her life has made me realize that she was a strong and independent woman, even while living with her parents. Although she became very independent, there were times, now that she was married, when she would consult her husband regarding certain situations or opportunities to get his thoughts on a particular matter.

For instance, there was a theater in St. Paul, on Maria between Conway and Third Streets, called "the De Luxe Theater," which showed silent movies.[45] Word got out that "the new gal in town," from Stillwater, Mildred (McLaggan) Brown was an excellent pianist who could play just about any song requested, as well as some spontaneous tunes that would go nicely with the silent movies.

Mildred and Fred didn't live too far from the theater and the manager was able to track her down. He asked her if she would be interested in a job as the pianist for the silent movies. She discussed this opportunity with her husband, and Fred wasn't too keen on the idea, as he believed a woman of her proper upbringing shouldn't be employed in that capacity, so Mildred declined. Fred was a successful St. Paul businessman who was a good provider for his family and perhaps wanted to make sure that his and his wife's lives wouldn't be misconstrued by the community by her having a job as a silent-film pianist.

This was 1920, and even though Mildred became a very independent woman in Stillwater and St. Paul before she was married, she was now the "Mrs." I know for a fact that she respected her husband and adored being his wife, a role she cherished and held very near and dear to her heart for thirty-eight years.

Another Wedding Wednesday Wedding

Dorothy McLaggan Photograph courtesy of Florence Jane Wennerberg, Mary Kirst and Jon Meister.

Dorothy, the fourth daughter born to John and Ivy McLaggan, was for many years the youngest daughter in the family, until Jean was born when Dorothy was fourteen.

Dorothy attended Stillwater High School, as did her sisters, where she met the man she would marry, Walter Lange.

The McLaggan household again prepared for a wedding, again scheduled for a weekday, another Wednesday. At the ages of twenty-six, Dorothy and Walter Lange were married on Wednesday, June 24, 1925, at St. Michael's Catholic Church, officiated by Father Charles Corcoran.

How curious it was for me to discover this interesting tradition, or dare I say, superstition, that many young couples adhered to in the past. The McLaggan parents, Ivy and John, were married on a Tuesday, their daughter Mildred

Walter Lange and Dorothy McLaggan Photograph Courtesy of Jon Meister

married Fred on a Wednesday, and it was again a Wednesday when Dorothy married Walter. A reason for a weekday wedding may have to do with an old folk rhyme, said to have originated in England, which reads as follows: [46]

Marry on Monday for health,
Tuesday for wealth,
Wednesday the best day of all,
Thursday for crosses,
Friday for losses,
and Saturday for no luck at all.

Remember, this is just an old folk rhyme and superstition that obviously has nothing to do with luck, as the family had their share of misfortunes throughout the years, even when the wedding occurred on a Tuesday or a Wednesday.

June 24 was an additional special day for the McLaggans, as it was also the mother of the bride's birthday. Ivy (Wright) McLaggan turned fifty-two the day her daughter, Dorothy, exchanged matrimonial vows with Walter Lange.

The wedding took place at the parish residence at three o'clock, p.m. The attendants were Miss Ruth Gillespie and Edward Fitzgerald.

The wedding announcement in the *Stillwater Gazette,* dated June, 25, 1925, states that a wedding dinner was served at the McLaggan household at 703 West Pine Street, immediately following the ceremony, for the bridal party and close relatives.

The newly married couple drove up to Duluth to board a boat to take them to Port Arthur, what is now Thunder Bay, Canada, for an extended honeymoon.

Dorothy and Walter didn't have any children; however, I always had the sense they had a great zeal for life. They had a love for nature and animals and would often go horseback riding at nearby stables in Washington County, or spend time together at local parks and lakes.

Dorothy also enjoyed music, and would inherit her grandfather Addison's fiddle. She occasionally played a bit of "chin music" for family and friends; however, she never became a professional musician like her grandfather.

Even though they didn't have children, the stories from Dorothy and Walter's nieces and nephews were that they were quite a fun pair to be around, and all enjoyed the time spent with the aunt and uncle.

Dorothy and Walter would be Stillwater residents for the rest of their lives.

Safely Home

After contracting influenza in 1919 during the pandemic, Florence was never the same, and she would have to fight for the strength to stay well over the years. Her sister Mildred and brother-in-law Fred would often take her to doctor appointments. They prayed she would have quick and full recoveries each time an illness would suddenly make an appearance and weaken her health. The two were happy to accompany Florence to her appointments, always wishing for the best.

In the early afternoon on June 26, 1926, Mildred was keeping a close watch over her sister, as she lay peacefully upon her bed. Florence was being comforted by her sister's blanket of love and tears when she breathed her last. Florence had succumbed to Encephalitis lethargica; a viral infection which would frequently impose itself upon her after she survived the influenza outbreak in 1919.[47]

This little woman of Stillwater was taken away from her parents and three sisters at the age of twenty-eight, seven years after they thought she defeated the predatory disease, which was relentless toward its surviving victims.

IN THE NEWS

Stillwater Gazette, June 9, 1926

Miss MacLaggan Called Home

Florence Rebecca, daughter of Mr. and Mrs. John A. MacLaggan, passed to the great beyond on Monday, June 7, after an illness of several months duration.

Miss MacLaggan was born and grew to womanhood in Stillwater where her beautiful character, her thoughtful, loving disposition have made her a host of friends who will learn with deepest regret of her early passing.

Besides her parents, she is survived by three sisters, Mrs. Frederick F. Brown, St. Paul; Mrs. Walter A. Lang, and Jean A., of Stillwater.

The funeral will be held on Wednesday morning at 9:30 from St. Michael's church, Rev. Chas. Corcoran officiating.

The obituary goes on to identify the pallbearers who lovingly carried Florence to her final resting place. They were several of her friends and a relative from Stillwater: Harry Madson, Walter Klein, Sherman McGee, Ralph McGrath, Bolton Gillespie, and her mother's second cousin, Joseph O'Brien.

Although her obituary states she died "after an illness of several months duration," her official Certificate of Death states, "Had recurring attacks following Influenza 1919."

Suddenly Without Her Sisters

Jean McLaggan was many years younger than her sisters. I often wonder if she ever felt that she missed out on the day-to-day activities and events her sisters experienced many years earlier before she was born when she heard stories of their get-togethers with their McLaggan cousins from Gordon, Wisconsin, or attending school together, or daily walks throughout the streets of Stillwater, or sharing favorite clothes, shoes, and accessories.

It's also the everyday mischief-making that siblings get into that make childhood memories unforgettable. However, I'm sure her sisters would include her in daily mischievousness just to tire their little sister out.

Even though Jean was the baby and many years younger than her sisters, the four were able to all live together for several years in the early years of Jean's life. Having her sisters leaving one by one due to different circumstances may have been difficult for the youngest McLaggan daughter. When Jean was seven, her sister Mildred married and left Stillwater to live in St. Paul for the rest of her life. When Jean was twelve, Dorothy married and left the family home to live with her husband. No doubt the hardest transition of all was when her sister Florence died when Jean was thirteen. Did these events make Jean feel a distance between herself and her older sisters? Not because they were many years apart in age, but because of the abruptness of losing the sister who remained at home with her after her two other sisters were married?

As Jean grew older, she had a strong bond with Mildred and Dorothy, regardless of the differences in their ages.

The Music Continues

The dedication to music continued to play a big part in the McLaggan family. Jean was very much involved with the music circles at Stillwater High School, as well as at St. Michael's, her family's parish. Beginning as a teen, in the late 1920s and early 1930s, she was part of the choir at St. Michael's, which she continued throughout adulthood.

As a young woman with the gift of a beautiful voice and musical ability, Jean was often one of the members of the choir whom when the director would point to, would be expected to perform an "on-the-spot" solo during elaborate performances.[48]

The choir director at that time was a man by the name of Claude D. Jackson. He was born in Stillwater in 1874 to Charles and Mattie Jackson. His father was a barber on Main Street. The family was identified as either "Negro" or black, depending on the source. Claude Jackson became a member of the choir at St. Michael's at the young age of fourteen, around 1888,[49] when Joseph L. Jones was St. Michael's organist and choir director.

Jean's Future Is on the Horizon

Jean was two years younger than the man she would marry. They may have met in high school, or perhaps at one of the stores her future father-in-law owned on Main Street over the years. His name was Merl Meister. He was born in Stillwater in 1911, and was the only child to Carl Meister and Clara (Kriesel) Meister.

Merl's father was born in Germany and migrated to the United States with his parents when he was very young. Merl's mother was born in 1872, also to parents of Germanic descent, and raised in Stillwater.

Merl's father was the proprietor of a few different stores on Main Street throughout the years. In the early 1900s, his father owned a saloon located at 254–256 South Main Street. After occupying that location for several years, his father opened a liquor and cigar store at 105 South Main Street.

When prohibition began, his father had to close his liquor store and opened a sporting goods store at 112 North Main Street. Some of the merchandise sold at the store was: fishing tackle, live bait, baseball goods, guns, ammunition, and cutlery, to name a few. He would offer the service of repairing sports equipment as well.

When prohibition ended, Carl Meister was once again able to open a liquor, cigar store, and tavern, known as "the store" by family members. The front of the store sold off-sale liquor and cigars. The tavern was at the other end, and cigars were made on the upper level.

The décor of the newly opened tavern had a sporting goods theme from some of the merchandise left over from the previous endeavor. There were fishing nets and poles, guns, and other sporting equipment adorning the walls of "the store."

Merl's father also organized a German band, which performed for a variety of celebrations and activities throughout the years.[50]

*T*he youngest McLaggan, Jean, and her future husband, Merl, both graduated from Stillwater High School in 1930 and 1931, respectively.

Merl's senior picture in the 1930 Kabekonian yearbook has his name spelled as "Merle Meister." Adjacent to his name is a list of clubs he was involved in, as well as his nickname and his senior quote. His nickname was "My." His senior quote is written as, "By studying my lady's eyes I've grown so learned day by day." He was in the Science Club, Thespians Club, participated in the senior play, and was also a member of the Hi-Y Club. The Hi-Y Club was a program established by the Young Men's Christian Association (YMCA), which encouraged high school boys to be involved in serving the community in order to create and maintain high moral character to the fullest capacity in their daily lives. [51]

Merl K. Meister
Photograph Courtesy of
Stillwater Public Library-
St. Croix Collection

Jean A. McLaggan
Photograph Courtesy of
Stillwater Public Library-
St. Croix Collection

After Merl graduated from high school, he furthered his studies taking some college courses in St. Paul, while he continued working for his father's store and tavern on Main Street.

Jean McLaggan graduated from Stillwater High School one year after her future husband. Next to her name and senior picture in the 1931 Kabekonian yearbook, is a list of the clubs she was involved in, and a senior quote. The lists include being a member of the Glee Club during all four years of high school, participating in her senior play; Shakespeare's Dream, Thespians Club, Science Club, Commercial Club, Talent Club, and the Girl Reserves, which was part of the Young Women's Christian Association (YWCA). The Girl Reserves began from informal gatherings, and the Patriotic League, both programs being associated with the YWCA. The Girl Reserves program was to assist young girls, between the ages of 12 to 18, in developing the best self they could be, while honoring their community, country, and God.[52] Her senior quote is written as; "With every minute you do change a mind."

Jean and Merl Are Wed

IN THE NEWS

The Stillwater Daily Gazette, June 17, 1936

Miss Jean McLaggan and Merl Meister are Wed

Mr. and Mrs. J.A. McLaggan announce the marriage of their daughter, Jean, to Merl Meister, son of Mr. and Mrs. Carl Meister of this city on June 17 . . .

Jean McLaggan and Merl Meister married at St. Michael's parsonage, on Wednesday, June 17, 1936. The weekday wedding custom in the McLaggan family was evidently an ongoing tradition, beginning with parents John and Ivy who married forty-two years earlier on a Tuesday, and both of Jean's sisters on a Wednesday—"Wednesday is the best day of all," according to the folk rhyme.

Jean and Merl's attendants on their special day were Jean's sister and brother-in-law, Dorothy and Walter Lange, and the officiant was none other than Father Charles Corcoran.

Their announcement in the Stillwater Gazette stated they would be going through the northern part of the state for their wedding trip, then reside in Stillwater.

Merl Meister and Jean McLaggan-Meister Photograph Courtesy of Jon Meister

After Jean and Merl were married, Merl continued to be employed by his father at Meister's Bar and Liquor Store, where he would eventually take over the business. The bar and liquor store, and the earlier sporting goods shop, at 112 North Main Street, would be the location of the family-owned businesses for over fifty years until closing in the mid-1980s.

A Special Announcement from Stillwater

*J*ean and Merl were both born and raised in Stillwater and lived there for most of their lives. They raised their five children in the historic neighborhood of Stillwater known as North Hill, at 212 West Cherry Street, built in 1872.

Their home on Cherry Street was surrounded by other historic homes and landmarks, just a couple blocks away from Pioneer Park, the property where lumber baron Isaac Staples built his mansion overlooking the river town during the logging era.

When Jean (McLaggan) Meister was getting ready to give birth for the third time in the early 1940s, having already given birth to a son, Jon, and a daughter, Martha, Jean's oldest sister was living in St. Paul, caring for a few of her own younger school-aged children. Mildred's daughters, Mary and Florence Jane, remember the day their twin cousins, Michael and Mary, were born in Stillwater. The St. Paul cousins were twelve and seven at the time, and say it was a day neither will ever forget.

It was a humid July day in St. Paul. Florence Jane was inside with their mother, Mary was outside talking to the neighbor, both standing on the respective sides of the fence. All of a sudden, their mother began shouting: "Twins were born! She had twins! Jean had twins!" She then proceeded to run out the front door, continuing to declare to the neighbors the news she just received from Stillwater about the arrival of her niece and nephew.

Mildred was usually a quiet woman, so her shouting with great excitement the news she had just received from her family in Stillwater was quite a surprise to her daughters, Mary and Florence Jane, and possibly their neighbors.

Jean and Merl had five children: Jon, Martha, twins Michael and Mary, and Tommy. This part of the collective family history, via the union between Jean McLaggan and Merl Meister, is still going strong in present-day Stillwater, as several generations of cousins continue to live there to carry on our family's legacy.

Paying Tribute to Father Corcoran

IN THE NEWS

The Stillwater Gazette, July 6, 1943

Hundreds Pay Tribute to Father Corcoran

The funeral Tuesday, of Very Reverend Father Corcoran, pastor of St. Michael's church, was one of the largest ever held in Stillwater.

Father Charles Corcoran, the honorable pastor at St. Michael's Catholic

Church for just over fifty years, went to his heavenly home on July 2, 1943. The article states his funeral was attended by a large crowd of people to bid him farewell, for he'd served three generations during his time at the parish.

Father Corcoran was a dependable holy servant to the McLaggan family, as well as for many others, when he officiated at weddings, baptisms, and funerals over the years. There were times when Father Corcoran would perform funeral rites for the very same Catholic Christians he had baptized as infants, something the McLaggans knew all too well. He was the priest in 1894 who officiated at Ivy Wright and John McLaggan's wedding, baptized all but one of their five daughters, performed two funeral rites for their daughters, Marguerite and Florence, and officiated at the weddings of daughters Mildred, Dorothy, and Jean.

Regardless of what Holy Sacrament Father Corcoran performed, the McLaggan Family would go on to cherish the meaningful heritage of the life of the Church he shared with them throughout the years of his ministry.

Father Charles Corcoran was laid to rest at St. Michael's Cemetery in Bayport, Minnesota.

Meanwhile, in St. Paul

*M*ildred and Fred Brown had six children together in St. Paul, born between the years 1920 and 1934: John Frederick, Marcus Joseph, Robert Louis, Mary Evelyn, Kenneth Addison, and Florence Jane. They raised their children at 1044 Hudson Avenue in St. Paul, near Earl Street, until the street's name was changed to Wilson Avenue around 1940, something the family wasn't too thrilled about at the time.

Throughout her life, Mildred was an independent woman. After her marriage, she was a stay-at-home mother, still independent, as she would very often be the one raising her and Fred's children on her own. Fred was a sales agent for the Great Northern Railroad and was traveling during most weeks, coming home on the weekends.

The couple helped their community whenever they could. During the

Great Depression and into the 1940s, when Fred returned from his weekly business travel, he and Mildred sat down at the kitchen table and had a conversation regarding the week's events in St. Paul. He asked his wife who in the neighborhood needed help, and they would put together a plan to distribute appropriate resources for the neighbors not as fortunate as they were.

One of the passions that Mildred brought with her to St. Paul from Stillwater was her love of music. She continued the tradition of filling her home with the echoing sounds of music and song, as she did while growing up and living in the same household for a while with her musician grandfather, Addison, on Olive Street.

The week the movie *The Bells of St. Mary's* opened in 1945, Mildred asked her daughter, Mary, if she would like to go along with her to see the movie starring Bing Crosby. Of course, Mary was elated when her mother invited her to come along. Mother and daughter absolutely loved the movie. The following day, Mary's mother asked her if she would again like to go to the same movie. Mary thought this was a bit strange as they just saw it the day before and the tickets were ten cents apiece! However, she agreed, and the two went to the theater and loved it the second time as much as the first. When they arrived home, her mother promptly sat down at the piano and began to play the song "The Bells of St. Mary's." It was the first time Mary had heard her mother play the song she had first heard in the movie theater. She now understood why her mother wanted to see the movie two days in a row. I suppose you could say it was for research purposes.

Mildred always welcomed the chance to accompany family and friends, or friends of her children, on her much-loved instrument, putting household chores aside any time the opportunity would arise. She would be willing to play any song they requested, often performing a song by ear after hearing just a few bars. That's one of the first things people remember about Mildred is that she was always willing and able to play the piano for anyone who was interested, needing only a suggestion for the music to begin.

During World War II, several of Mildred and Fred's sons were in the armed forces. Their son, Bob, was enlisted in the Navy. Prior to shipping out, Bob brought a few extra enlisted men to his family home in St. Paul.

Many neighbors knew of the upcoming visit and were anxiously awaiting the service men's arrival. They sat on their front porches and lawns, or looked out their windows as they waited for the taxicab to be in sight. When the taxi arrived at the Wilson Avenue home, the doors "sailed" open, and out came Mildred and Fred's son, Bob, followed by a crew of three or four young sailors in uniform, piling out of the cab as quickly as possible. Each one tried to outrun the next, laughing anxiously as they heard a group of neighbors cheering for them, from their lawns and front porches.

The young men in uniform who were lucky enough to be a guest at their friend's childhood home, heard how their friend's mother loved playing the piano and would welcome anyone that would like to sing along. The younger siblings of the brothers in uniform remember a few times when some of their brothers' military friends would come home with them to experience a little bit of sweet "home away from home." The sisters and brothers would surround the piano and sing like there was no tomorrow, watching their mother as she enjoyed her favorite pastime. If Mildred didn't know a song, the requester would sing a few bars and she'd begin to play it as if she knew it all her life.

One particular man in uniform asked Mildred if she knew the song "Ramona," a 1928 song by L. Wolfe Gilbert and Mabel Wayne. It was a favorite of his, as it shared the name of the girlfriend he was missing. Mildred knew the song by ear and began to play it, while he sang along to her accompaniment. Mildred's young daughters, Mary and Florence Jane, remember seeing a gentle tear run slowly down his cheek as he finished up his solo.

These military troubadours would sing for hours, only breaking for the dinner Mildred had whipped together for them, which included her famous chocolate cake. They would then take up at the piano again for as long as they could, until it was time for the yellow cab to collect them and bring them back to reality.

Singing, smiling, and laughing, these men in uniform were taken away from their thoughts and impending experiences of World War II for a few hours that seemed like minutes, in a loving family home on the East Side of St. Paul, where music was its theme.

Aunt Do Do's Candy Shop

There are two notable memories that Aunt Dorothy is best known for in the family. The first was her nickname. She was affectionately known as Aunt Do Do, pronounced as "Doe Doe," by her nieces and nephews. This nickname continues to this day when speaking of her. The second notable memory was that she worked at a candy shop. It was magical to hear the stories of how she had the luck of being surrounded by all the wonderful, enticing sweets the candy and confection shop had to offer.

Dorothy (McLaggan) Lange was the manager of the very popular local shop Goggin's Candy, owned by J.A. Goggin. In addition to the candy that she presented so beautifully in each case, there was also a nut roasting machine with a variety of nuts, which were still warm when she handed the customer their bag full of cashews, almonds, pecans, and more. Aunt Do Do became a recognizable citizen of Stillwater because of her genuine and kind demeanor while standing behind the counter, assisting customers on the days they visited to indulge in a little bit of the famous candy.

During the mid-1940s, near the end of World War II, Aunt Do Do would send for her young nephew, Jon, who lived at 212 West Cherry Street, to come to the store so he could run some errands for her. When Jon arrived at the shop on Main Street, Aunt Do Do would hand him several securely wrapped packages of specially selected Goggin's candies. Jon carried the precious boxes full of goodies to the Stillwater post office. These boxes of sweet love and appreciation would be mailed off and delivered to soldiers serving around the world during the war. I can only imagine the delight on the soldiers' faces when they received a box of the delicious hand-chosen candies from a small-town candy shop on Main Street in Stillwater, Minnesota.

As Aunt Do Do never had any children, it was quite fitting for her to spoil her nieces and nephews. She had a total of eleven, five in Stillwater and six in St. Paul, during the time she managed Goggin's. She had very good and enjoyable relationships with all of them. She would see her nieces and nephews from Stillwater very often, as they didn't live too far from each other; she lived on South Second Street, while they lived about a mile away on Cherry Street.

Her nieces and nephews from her oldest sister, Mildred, who lived in St. Paul, loved going to visit their mother's historic hometown, knowing that a visit to Aunt Do Do's candy shop would be on the agenda for the day, in addition to visiting their McLaggan grandparents, their aunt Jean, and their cousins.

***Dorothy McLaggan-Lange at Goggin's
Candy Shop, Stillwater, MN
Photograph Courtesy of Jon Meister***

CHAPTER THIRTEEN

The Adored Grandparents

John and Ivy McLaggan were like celebrities to their eleven grandchildren. This is how I have grown to know who my great-grandparents were, because of all the special memories and stories that were handed down from their grandchildren. Each grandchild had the same opinion about their grandparents, knowing them as loving, wonderful, proper, gentlemanly, and very pleasant to be around. They were the set of grandparents everyone wanted to have, and some of their grandchildren's friends actually made that statement.

St. Paul Grandsons, John "Jack" and Marcus "Bud" Brown, circa 1926 Courtesy of Florence Jane Wennerberg

The grandchildren from St. Paul remember with great fondness how excited they were to know they were going to visit their grandparents for a week or two when school let out for the summer. This was a big adventure for them during the 1930s and 1940s. Packing for the extended vacation the night before their departure was like getting ready for Christmas. They often had difficulty sleeping the night before, as they imagined themselves walking around the "old-fashioned" town, and up and down the "never-ending" steps, beginning at the top of South Broadway Street and ending on Main Street. During their visits, they would easily walk down the many steps to Main Street without stopping. Their destination would be Goggin's or, as it was known to the family, Aunt Do Do's Candy Shop. Visiting with their aunts, and their grandparents' neighborhood friends was an event they always looked forward to, wondering if their names would appear in the *Stillwater Gazette* to announce their visit, which happened on occasion.

When their midday adventure to downtown was complete, the grandchildren would begin their ascent of the one hundred-plus steps, beginning on Main Street to the top of Broadway. Their return ascent, which consisted of many more stops, usually took much longer than their descent.

Today, the stairs at South Main Street is a popular landmark and destination for exercise enthusiasts, and consists of 157 concrete steps.

The Grandchildren Visit St. Michael's

During the grandchildren's visits to their grandparents' home, Ivy, whom the grandchildren referred to as "Nana," had them attend Mass with her at St. Michael's Catholic Church, where she and her mother's family, the Tobins, were parishioners.

On their way to church, Ivy relayed to her grandchildren that in the early years of St. Michael's, sometime after it was built on Third and Walnut Streets, to help support the parish, the parishioners had the opportunity to rent their own private pew for Mass. When she was raising her daughters, they were one of the parishioner families who did so.[53] The McLaggans' reserved pew had a small plaque attached to it with their name written upon it, designating it the McLaggan's private pew. In addition to the plaque naming the family it "belonged" to, there was a wooden gate that closed after the family occupied their pew to begin to prepare for Holy Mass.

Upon entering the church, after sharing this story, Ivy escorted her grandchildren up the aisle to find an available row, and gently guided them into a now unreserved pew. Grandmother and grandchildren quietly took their seats and listened to Holy Mass in Latin.

Fishing with Grandpa

*J*ohn McLaggan, who wasn't Catholic, would occasionally attend Mass with his wife and grandchildren; however, he enjoyed a different way spending time with his grandchildren. During their visits, he often took them on long walks down to the St. Croix River and stayed there for hours at a time, fishing.

Grandson Michael from Stillwater remembers the anticipation he endured while waiting for his grandfather to open his tackle box and allow him to look through its collection of fine fishing lures. When John unlatched his treasure chest full of bait, he explained to Michael the correct ones to use to catch certain fish, and which ones should be used for the best of luck on any given day. Michael still has some of the treasured lures that his grandfather John gave to him during the many days of fishing.

Grandson Jon from Stillwater remembers a time he accompanied his grandparents, along with Aunt Do Do, for days full of fishing, swimming, and relaxing, when they stayed at a cabin on Lake Carnelian, which is a nearby lake about eight miles to the north of downtown Stillwater. At the time, the lake was a vacation destination for many Minnesota residents. Today, Lake Carnelian has mostly residential homes surrounding its shores, with a few smaller vacation homes squeezed in-between.

Christmas Time

"*A*ll I wanted for Christmas was for our grandparents from Stillwater to be with us on Christmas Day" was the sentiment remembered by the McLaggans' granddaughter Mary Evelyn. She said she would be more excited about her grandparent's arrival at her home in St. Paul than

St. Paul granddaughter, Mary Brown, circa 1932 Photograph courtesy of Mary Kirst and Dianne Shutt

opening presents on Christmas morning. On Christmas Day, she would anxiously wait upon her parents' bed, looking out their second-story bedroom window while anticipating the approaching car of her grandparents from Stillwater, or seeing them appear over the hill after taking the bus from Stillwater to St. Paul.

Stillwater Grandchildren; Jon, Martha, Michael, Mary and Tommy Meister, circa 1947 Photograph courtesy of Jon Meister

The grandchildren born in Stillwater would eventually have the pleasure of Christmases with their grandparents. The Stillwater grandchildren were younger than their St. Paul cousins, so when the Stillwater cousins were being added to the family, it was much easier for the elderly grandparents to travel less than a mile to Jean's home on Cherry Street.

They Were Wonderful!

John McLaggan's car, which grandson Jon identified as a black Stearns-Knight, would always have a supply of round mints readily available. However, Jon never helped himself to the tempting treats unless his grandfather offered. Both Jon and Michael from Stillwater never minded the chores or work they were given around their Nana and grandfather's Stillwater home, as a freshly baked lemon meringue pie would be waiting for them as payment when they finished.

Granddaughter Florence Jane, born in St. Paul, remembers her grandmother Ivy's talent for needlepoint and sewing, and said Ivy would often sew aprons for her and her sister, Mary. One of her needlepoint masterpieces was of *The Last Supper,* today adorning a wall in a great-granddaughter's home.

Kenneth Addison, a grandson from St. Paul, summed up his grandparents from Stillwater in a brief, to the point statement: "They were wonderful!"

Regardless, of where the grandchildren resided, they all shared similar and endearing stories about their much-loved grandparents, Ivy and John McLaggan.

St. Paul Grandson, Robert "Bob" Brown, circa 1944 Photograph courtesy of Mary Jean Brown

IN THE NEWS

Fifty-Fifth Wedding Anniversary

The Stillwater Gazette, September 12, 1949

Host of Friends Greet MacLaggans On 55th Anniversary

Mr. and Mrs. John A. MacLaggan welcomed close to 200 guests Sunday afternoon, Sept. 11, at the Merl Meister home on the occasion of their fifty-fifth wedding anniversary . . .

According to the article in the *Stillwater Gazette*, the lovely celebration was adorned with "a color scheme of dusty pink and white with a touch of emerald green."

Ivy and John were lucky enough to have celebrated many years together. On September 11, 1949, after fifty-five years of marriage, their daughter Jean and her husband, Merl, hosted a special anniversary party at 212 West Cherry Street.

John and Ivy definitely had their share of experiences, including much joy and sorrow over the years. However, they continued to embrace the love of their growing family and were excited to share their special anniversary of fifty-five years together with family and friends in the town where they had grown to adulthood.

They celebrated their fifty-fifth anniversary with their three daughters, Mildred, Dorothy, and Jean, and their families. Their five Stillwater grandchildren, aged from seven to twelve, also assisted during the celebration. Mildred and Fred were also present with their six children from St. Paul, with ages ranging from fifteen to twenty-nine years old. At the time of their anniversary, Ivy and John also had a great-grandson, two-year-old John Patrick, from their eldest grandchild, John (Jack), from St. Paul.

Those assisting with the managing of the party at the Cherry Street "venue" were friends and acquaintances such as E.F. Curran, Gustav B. Glasrud, Ruth Josewski, Harold Chatterton, R.E. Nelson, Don Monty, Mary Henley, Pearl Reiland, J. H. Haines, Frank Johnson, E.M. Mosier, and Margaret Benham.

Some of the other guests that were present during the celebration that day, as stated in the *Stillwater Gazette*, were: Mr. and Mrs. Pothen, Edward Loney and family, Mary Jean Holmberg, Lois Brisson, Donald Kirst, and Martin Brown.

John and Ivy deeply appreciated the recognition by their friends and family, who knew of the love, joy, and sorrow they experienced through the many years of their lives together.

***St. Paul Grandson,
Kenneth Addison
Brown, Okinawa,
circa 1951
Photograph courtesy
of Kenneth A. Brown
and Cheryl Crosser***

***St. Paul
granddaughter,
Florence Jane
Brown, circa 1944
Photograph courtesy
of Florence Jane
Wennerberg and
Julie Youngberg***

CHAPTER FOURTEEN

Dorothy McLaggan-Lange
A.K.A. Aunt Do Do

Aunt Do Do's grand-nieces and grand-nephews who visited Goggin's Candy in the early 1950s and early 1960s, recount their visits as very memorable experiences. After their parents found a place to park on Main Street near the candy store, the children couldn't get out of the car fast enough. They walked through the entrance to the candy shop, experiencing an overload of sweetness and beauty combined. Walking around from the back to the front of the counter, Aunt Do Do appeared, greeting the two generations of nieces and nephews with hugs and kisses for all. Their memories of her are of her pleasant, upbeat personality.

On their visits to the candy shop, Aunt Do Do treated them to whatever candies they wanted. She handed them each a small white paper bag and instructed them to take their time and view each and every candy case full of the beautifully displayed treats. Her young grand-nieces and nephews accepted her statement to the utmost extent, as they knew whatever Aunt Do Do said in her magical candy shop basically trumped whatever "candy rule" of Mom and Dad's.

Even though she was manager of the shop and never owned it, when family members speak of Goggin's store, it is always referred to as "Aunt Do Do's candy shop."

When Aunt Do Do died unexpectedly in 1963, it wasn't just a surprise for family and close friends, but for the community as a whole, as she was a very well-known and well-liked person from the candy shop on Main Street.

Excerpt from the *Stillwater Messenger, October 21, 1963*

Dorothy A. Lange, Manager Of Party Shop Here, Dies

Mrs. Dorothy A. Lange for many years manager of the Goggin party shop in Stillwater, died Saturday afternoon . . .

Her unexpected death caused wide sorrow in the community where she had resided her entire life. She had been manager of the Goggin shop since its establishment.

Four of her loving nephews, and husbands of two of her nieces, carried Dorothy to her final resting place next to her husband, Walter, and her parents, John and Ivy, in the MacLaggan Family Plot in Stillwater's Fairview Cemetery.

Excerpt from the *Stillwater Messenger, October 22, 1963*

Requiem mass for Mrs. Dorothy Lang was sung Tuesday morning at 9 a.m. At St. Michael's Catholic church.

Casket bearers were Jon, Tom and Mike Meister, Donald Kirst, Kenneth Brown, and Russel Juhl.

CHAPTER FIFTEEN

Mildred McLaggan-Brown

Through the Eyes of a Child

Throughout her life, Mildred continued being an independent and caring woman, a characteristic she developed early in life. After five of their six children grew to adulthood, married and began families of their own, Mildred and Fred, along with their teenaged daughter Florence Jane, moved to a smaller home at 1348 East Third Street, in St. Paul. After their move to the Third Street home, she volunteered her time for the Sisters of St. Joseph of Carondelet; at the time, the convent was associated with St. Pascal's Church at White Bear Avenue and Third Street in St. Paul. She either walked or took the bus a little less than a mile to the convent and prepared daily meals for the nuns.

Mildred (McLaggan) Brown from Stillwater is a celebrated role model for her granddaughters of all generations, myself included. A woman of few words, she was more often silent than conversational. She was proper like her mother, Ivy (Wright) McLaggan. If she were to speak to one of my sisters or me, it was to ask to assist her with something, which we were always willing to do. Sometimes it would be to help her stir the custard filling she prepared for the scrumptious eclairs she would occasionally make on her Sunday visits.

While I sat next to her on the couch, she would ask for help to thread a sewing needle, as she could no longer see its opening. On Christmas Eve, she would ask one of us, or one of our cousins, to help her refasten her holiday pin that became loose from her wool coat after being at the bottom of a heap of winter coats thrown haphazardly upon my parents' bed during our annual Christmas Eve party.

The way she liberated herself from silence was by playing the piano. She is the only person I have ever personally known that was able to take command of the keys in a way that seemed effortless. The memory and sound of her playing the piano at my childhood home in St. Paul is still very clear in my mind, just as the melody she played, and lyrics of "Glow Worm," sung by the Mills Brothers, is like a recent memory: "Shine little glow-worm glimmer, glimmer . . ."

I can still hear her voice when I would answer the phone when she called:

"Hello?"

Grandma's response, "Mary?"

"No, Grandma, it's, Terri."

"Will you get your mother, please?"

"Ok, just a minute, please."

I tried to be proper with my grandmother on or off the phone; she had that way about her that made you want to be appropriate with her. If my mother wasn't available right away, I would go back to my phone call with Grandma and try my best to stretch the conversation as long as possible.

"Grandma, my mom can't talk right now, but I'll talk with you until she can. How are you?"

"Oh, I'm fine."

. . . pause . . . pause. . .pause . . .

I continued, "How's Kitty?"

"Oh, he's fine."

. . . pause . . . pause . . . pause.

"Okay, here's my mom, bye Grandma."

"Bye-bye."

And I handed the phone to my mom.

Grandma, a woman of few words, unless there was something of importance for her to share or wanted us to remember. Through the eyes of a child, I saw her as a typical, kind, and quiet grandma. Through the eyes of an adult, I now see her as a resilient, confident, independent, and caring woman, and I know this to be true after researching her life's story.

Grandma Brown—the formal way in which her grandchildren addressed her—was very proper and only spoke when spoken to; however, she was definitely not a pushover. She acquired confidence from a very early age, not afraid of going where she was needed or to take on a new challenge or adventure. You wouldn't have realized the courage that lay beneath her "grandma" looks when you first met her, or maybe ever, because she was so quiet and unassuming. She never bragged or spoke about herself; everyone else would do that for her. However, there were times when she remembered these sensitive and moving stories and relayed them to my family and me, breaking her silence for brief moments. This has helped me understand where her strength in life came from.

When I began researching my family, I shared her sadness and confusion when her baby sister, Marguerite, died, and I was overcome with sadness and emotion when reading the words about her sister Florence's death. Although we were generations apart, my emotions were in present time, and I wanted to be there for my grandma. She obviously held it together all those years of me knowing her, as I didn't know the extent of her losses until many years later. Is this the reason she was so quiet? Maybe the daily chatter of life wasn't meaningful enough for her after the certain experiences she had endured. I know the majority of her life was a good and wonderful life, although it was sprinkled with sorrow; she persevered. As I now recognize her as a role model, I believe the key to her happiness was the relationships she shared with her parents and sisters, which she ultimately carried through to new generations after she was married and had children of her own. My grandma, Mildred (McLaggan) Brown, may have been a woman of few words, but her actions and silence spoke volumes.

CHAPTER SIXTEEN

Jean McLaggan-Meister

The Tradition of Music Continues

The tradition of music that began in the family with Addison Wright, continued throughout the years in the McLaggan family. Jean (McLaggan) Meister continued to be a member of St. Michael's choir throughout her life. In addition to singing in the choir, she also sang for weddings, memorial Masses, and funerals.

From the years 1943 to 1968, Father Francis Miller was pastor at St. Charles Catholic Church in Bayport, Minnesota, then later became pastor at St. Michael's in Stillwater. He was also chaplain at the Stillwater State prison, located in Bayport, Minnesota; a position he held for forty years.[54,55] Jean was one of the several choir members of St. Michael's whom Father Miller would ask to accompany him and lead songs during Mass at the prison. For many years, Jean and the choir would participate during Mass with Father Miller, encouraging the inmates to sing along while worshiping. At the conclusion of each Mass, Father Miller and the melodious messengers of God were treated to a wonderful breakfast at the prison, something they looked forward to each time.

Due to his selfless acts of kindness, Father Miller developed a good rapport and meaningful relationships with the inmates, guiding them along in their faith. He referred to these inmates as "my boys" and "my angels with dirty faces." For many years, some of them served alongside Father Miller, assisting him on the altar during Mass.

When Father Miller died on December 31, 1968, due to complications from a fall on Christmas morning while on his way to say Mass for his "boys," the inmates who were close to him felt the immense loss from his passing. As the inmates were unable to attend his funeral at St. Michael's, they requested that Father Miller be able to lay in state at the prison so they could pay their respects. Their request was granted, and on January 1, 1969, in a reverent and orderly fashion, his "angels with dirty faces" walked past his casket and said their final goodbyes to their beloved messenger of God. Services for Father Miller at the State Prison also included a requiem Mass and an ecumenical service.[56]

Marine on St. Croix

Besides having the love of music deep within her soul, Jean loved nature and being outdoors. After Jean and Merl lived on Cherry Street and raised their family, they purchased a home in Marine on St. Croix. The home was stylishly beautiful, as was the property where it sat. I liken their property to a peaceful retreat, with an abundance of trees and a gently flowing creek running through, where watercress and morel mushrooms grew.

Jean loved sharing her property with the birds and forest animals, whom she would greet each day when providing them their morning seeds, suet, and salt blocks set out for the deer who appreciated their nature-loving neighbors.

Christmas Music, Cookies, and More

It wouldn't be a traditional family Christmas without the presence of music within the McLaggan/Meister household.

Jean and Merl inherited their musical talents; beginning with Jean, from her grandfather Addison and Uncle Addy, and Merl from his father Carl Meister, who organized the German Band in Stillwater. For many years, Jean continued the tradition of music within her family and for her grandchildren, who would converge upon their grandparents' home for their traditional

Christmas feast and celebration. Her family loved seeing her enjoying herself, as she outdid herself not only with the music she presented, but with her Christmas decorations as well. These were pre-HGTV, pre-Martha Stewart, and definitely worthy of the comparison.

The Christmas tree she decorated looked as though she took it directly from the cover of a current-day Christmas magazine. The holiday tables were elaborately decorated and reminiscent of a Victorian Christmas. They were intricately adorned for the family of all ages to enjoy, complete with pewter and crystal goblets, and fancy silverware set gracefully next to each place setting.

Before her grandchildren arrived for their Christmas celebration, Jean would carefully set their stockings on the stairs that led to the upper level of her home. The stockings were arranged oldest to youngest, beginning with the highest step for the oldest grandchild's stocking, to the lowest step for the youngest. The stockings were overflowing with small gifts; an apple and orange would also be included for each recipient.

One of the most memorable Christmas traditions Jean took on, besides the unforgettable music and home decorating, was when she would bake and decorate many dozens of ornate cookies to present to family and friends, near and far. Her cookies were not your typical cookies, as they are remembered by many as works of art.

Jean was a very artistic and creative woman. My family in St. Paul was lucky enough to have our great-aunt Jean hand-deliver these unforgettable "oh-so fragile, window-display" type of cookies herself.

It's hard to imagine the amount of time and effort she took to roll out the sugar cookie dough to the exact thickness each and every time before the designated cookie cutter would make its appearance to create individual "sweet-canvases." While the cookies cooled, she created the most perfect consistency of icings of several colors, and hand-painted each individual cookie. She added tiny ribbons and bows, delicate bells, and other petite decorations to finish off her intricate and edible works of art. Her grandchildren all struggled with the idea of eating them, but when they would bring themselves to do so they realized they tasted as good as they looked.

Nature's Beauty and Sound

Jean and her husband enjoyed many days with their family on the river, often boating up the St. Croix to Taylor's Falls, Minnesota. The nature-loving boaters took in the natural beauty Minnesota has to offer with its abundance of trees, picturesque falls, and pastel-painted skies.

On many warm summer evenings, when dusk was slowly transitioning into a quiet, tepid night, Jean enjoyed spending time on their houseboat, while docked on the St. Croix River. Very often she drifted off to sleep by its slight rocking motion, not waking until the next morning, being comforted by a blanket of stars while listening to the quiet melodies from nature's tiniest fiddlers, reminiscent of music from generations past.

Welcoming the New Descendants

My grandmother's youngest sister Jean and her husband Merl, were often present for a variety of parties or special days in my childhood home; baptisms, first communions, graduations, Christmas cookie delivery day, etc. Aunt Jean always went out of her way to make my sisters and me feel special. This became even more apparent after my grandmother, Jean's eldest sister, Mildred died in 1974.

My mother was Jean's niece and my sisters and I were her grandnieces. I have many fond memories of times I spent with my great-aunt Jean. One in particular is when my first child, my son Andy, was born.

Andy was born at St. Joseph's Hospital, the same hospital where my mother and I, as well as my second son, Chris, were all born. It's a multi-generational hospital for my family from St. Paul.

During the late 1970s and early 1980s, a new mother usually stayed in the hospital for up to three days. Two days after Andy's birth I was feeling very emotional. I was holding him in my arms looking at this beautiful creation

God had bestowed upon me. His face was perfect and free of any blemish. He had just a touch of pink on his cheeks. His eyes were barely open but I could still see the beautiful shade of blue. I had a limited view of the snowy January day through the hospital window, as I had the curtain closed halfway around my bed. All I wanted was to be alone with my newborn son and keep him warm in my arms—imagining the cold air as I saw the snow flurries flying by my window.

I heard soft footsteps of someone entering my room. The last person I wanted to see was a nurse trying to bring my baby back to the nursery, or poke me with another needle of some sort. As the curtains were slowly drawn open, my great-aunt Jean suddenly appeared—smiling at me with a gift for my baby boy. I wanted to greet her with a smile, then unexpectedly, I began to cry. All at once, she had a look of compassion and concern on her face. She came close to me and told me everything would be okay and that I had the baby blues. She said many mothers get "the blues" after giving birth, and I would be fine in no time. She continued smiling and began to ask me questions about my new son and how he was doing. She gave me bits of advice, keeping the conversation going along, obviously to keep my mind off of the "baby blues."

It still amazes me to think my great-aunt Jean made the effort and traveled over 30 miles from Marine on St. Croix to a hospital in downtown St. Paul, on a cold winter January day, to meet her newly born great-grandnephew just because she wanted to.

These special visits were something her son Jon told me were very important to her. It was a family tradition she was happy to continue over the years. This example portrayed by my great-aunt Jean has been a lasting tradition held by the family. No matter when, where, or how they have arrived, many of us continue this practice—to welcome the new descendants into the family.

Three Family Trees Become One
Birth and death years not appearing in this family tree
can be found in earlier chapters per family.

The Tobins
The Wrights
The McLaggans

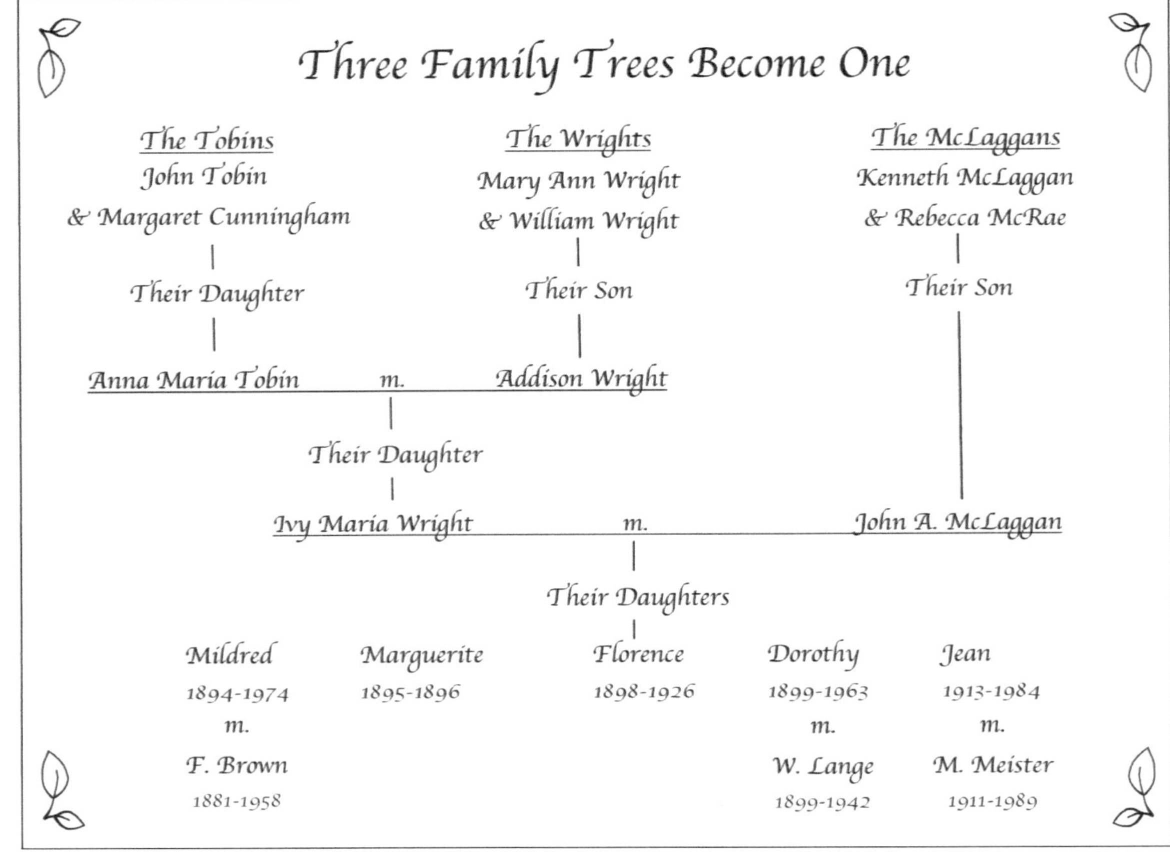
Three Family Trees Become One

The Tobins
John Tobin
& Margaret Cunningham

Their Daughter

Anna Maria Tobin   m.   Addison Wright

The Wrights
Mary Ann Wright
& William Wright

Their Son

The McLaggans
Kenneth McLaggan
& Rebecca McRae

Their Son

Their Daughter

Ivy Maria Wright   m.   John A. McLaggan

Their Daughters

Mildred
1894-1974
m.
F. Brown
1881-1958

Marguerite
1895-1896

Florence
1898-1926

Dorothy
1899-1963
m.
W. Lange
1899-1942

Jean
1913-1984
m.
M. Meister
1911-1989

CLOSING REMARKS

They Were Pioneers

Today, over 160 years from when my family first settled in Stillwater in the 1850s, there is a certain feeling that at times overwhelms me when I think of what I have learned about them and some of the struggles they endured. I'm sure it has much to do with what I felt while I was reading the words in the various documents regarding their lives. "They were pioneers"—a familiar phrase that will always hold a special place in my heart, the phrase my mother would say over and over again when relaying stories about our family who migrated to Stillwater.

The closeness I have developed with many of these ancestors, most of whom I never met, remains with the unspoken words I continue to discover or from the stories I've heard from the family that knew them best.

When I go online to look at the various websites on Stillwater, or the several Facebook pages honoring the city, to view all the beautiful pictures of the enchanting town of my ancestors, I'm drawn to their logo, which reads, "Discover Stillwater," . . . and that's exactly what I did.

Generations of Grandchildren

If it wasn't for Ivy (Wright) and John McLaggan's two daughters Mildred and Jean marrying their respective husbands and having eleven children between the two of them, our pioneer history from Stillwater would have quickly faded away.

Even though our McLaggan family name has somewhat disappeared over the years, due to John and Ivy having only daughters, their descendants have not.

The Eleven Grandchildren of Ivy Wright and John McLaggan

St. Paul Grandchildren

John Frederick, Marcus Joseph, Robert Louis, Mary Evelyn, Kenneth Addison, and Florence Jane

Stillwater Grandchildren

Jon Karl, Martha Jean, Michael William, Mary Wright, and Thomas

The following names of the great-grandchildren of several generations are not in chronological order; rather, they are grouped by families in order of the eleven grandchildren of Ivy and John McLaggan.

Great-Grandchildren

St Paul Descendants

John Patrick • Steve • Mark, Katie, Keith, Sheila, Brian • Frances, Susan, Mary Jo, Laurie, Theresa, Dianne • Colleen, Scott, Karen, Daniel, Paul, Cheryl • Michael, Patti Jo, Jeanne, Maribeth, Michelle, Julie, and Dan

Stillwater Descendants

Jeffrey, Bradley, Rebecca, Molly • Susan, Amiee • Michael, Lee, and Jean

Great-Great-Grandchildren

St. Paul Descendants

Amy, Lynn • Aaron, Ashley • Hillary, Mary Frances, Brian, Meghan, Adam, Michael, Caitlin • Allen, Angie, Cody, Lisa, Sean, Heather, Travis, Anthony, Nicholas, Jenna, Andrew, Christopher, Meghan, Kirsti, Jake • Nicole, Angie, Brooke, Keri, Melissa, Jeremy, Jason, Jenny, Eric, Aaron, Sam, Max, Laurel, Julia, Ryan, Nate, Emalee • John, Christine, James, Brent, Katherine, Aaron, Alyssa, Kayla, Blake, Corbin, Kameron, and Dane

Stillwater Descendants

Michael, Joseph, Kayla, Sam, Jessica, Emily, Anna, Luke, Diego, Ellie • Amelia, Molly • Dannielle, Austin, Jessica, Justin, Hunter, and Brendan

Great-Great-Great-Grandchildren

St. Paul Descendants

Ryan, Tyler, Ian, Tia, Reece • Emma, Hayes • Jackson, Brooklyn, Sabrina, Sean, Lydia, Janey, Jett, Brady, Mason, Travis, Aidan, Adalynn, Eddie, Evelyn, Elayna, Carter, Ella, Shaeyna, Kyliee, Nick, Landon, Liam, Josh, Henry, Ben, Luke • McKenzie, Jack, Charley, Finn, Taylor, Henry, Addison, Alyssa, Jackson, Riley, Billy, Wesley • Daisy, Johnny, Gemma, Jameson, and Cole

Stillwater Descendants

Mia Rose, David, Madison and Mabel Mae

APPENDICES

Appendix A

Familiar Faces

The similarity of features of some past relatives compared to present day relatives seems almost mysterious, especially when there is more than one hundred years between them.

The following two brothers, six years apart from each other, and cousins of different generations to the many descendants listed in this book, are 115 and 121 years apart respectively, from their great-great-grandfather, John Alexander McLaggan.

John McLaggan, circa 1890

*John "Mugs" • A great-great
Grandson of John A. McLaggan*

*James • A great-great
Grandson of John A. McLaggan*

Appendix B

Select Obituaries

In the introduction of this book, I wrote how the text of an obituary at times assisted me when writing about my ancestors' lives. This method may also assist future researchers interested in creating a family narrative. Included in this appendix are a few select obituaries for examples.

After reading the following obituaries, you will be able to recognize how they were of significant help to me and became one of the main sources I relied on when writing a creative story about a family member.

The Stillwater Gazette, June 18, 1893

Death of Professor J.L. Jones

Contrary to the hopeful and expectations of the family and friends of Mr. Jones, who were led to believe yesterday that possible recovery might reasonably be expected, the patient last evening established more unfavorable symptoms, and about 10 o'clock seized with a sinking spell from which it seemed impossible to rally. Medical skill was of no avail, and a few minutes after 11 o'clock, the end came, and the sufferer closed his weary eyes in death.

Calmly, as to a night's repos,

Or flowers at set o' sun.

Mr. Jones seemed to have, from the first attack about two weeks ago, a premonition that for him, life's record was to be closed.

He bore up bravely, notwithstanding, but the symptoms steadily became more alarming, and the patient slowly sank until death relieved his suffering.

The funeral will take place from the family residence, No. 515 South Third street, at 3:30 o'clock to-morrow (Sunday) afternoon, under the auspices of the Odd Fellows Lodge of this city, of which society deceased was an active and valued member.

Joseph Lyman Jones was born in the township of Burns, Alleghany county N.Y., Feb 24, 1828, and was consequently in the 66th year of his age. From infancy he was afflicted with imperfect eyesight, and his parents removing to Ohio while he was a boy, the child was placed in the Blind Institute at Columbus, where he received a thorough education. He was married to Sarah N. Chapman in Painesville, Ohio, who died in 1858, and in 1858 he married Mrs. Mary A. Wright of Chicago, who survives him, with her two grown-up children, Addison Wright and Mrs. Will. Harper. He was a member of the band connected with the Fourth Wisconsin Infantry, but was discharged at the expiration of about a year on account of failing eyesight. He resided in Hudson several years, removing to this city about 25 years ago, and has all these years followed his profession of teacher of music. He was a most exemplary man in all the walks of life, and his many noble traits of manliness, honor and integrity endeared him to relatives, neighbors and the community in which he lived, all of whom deeply mourn the loss of an esteemed and honored citizen.

The Stillwater Gazette; Front Page, October 3, 1900

Kenneth MacLaggan Passes Away Unexpectedly at a West Superior Hotel.

Kenneth MacLaggan, a respected citizen of Stillwater died suddenly yesterday afternoon at the Richelieu hotel in West Superior. The announcement of his death came to this city in a telegram about 10 o'clock last night. Having been a man of robust health the news of his death came as a great surprise to relatives and friends.

He went to bed in the hotel Thursday night in the best of health. Not appearing yesterday about the hotel, the cause of his absence was investigated and he was found dead in bed at 8 o'clock last evening. His death was doubtless due to heart failure thus ending a useful life unexpectedly. Mr. MacLaggan had gone to West Superior on business and intended to leave this morning for Gordon, Wis. He carried his heavy grip to the hotel from the train, refusing the offer of another to carry it, and claiming that he was able to wait upon himself in such respects.

Deceased was 65 years old. He was born in New Brunswick and came to Stillwater 33 years ago. For many years he logged on the St. Croix upon his own responsibility but for the past thirteen years has been in the employ of the Musser-Sauntry company, looking after their camps in the capacity of foreman, purchasing horses, outfits and camp supplies. He was on his way from the State Line camps of that company to Gordon when death ended his career.

He was married in New Brunswick before coming to this city to Miss Rebecca McRae. Surviving him are the widow, and four grown children, they being: John A. MacLaggan, of this city, Kenneth W. MacLaggan, a resident of West Superior; Miss Eva R. MacLaggan, principal of the Nelson school, and Robert [Roderick] H. MacLaggan who makes his home here but spends much of his time in logging camps.

Mr. MacLaggan was a contractor in this city for several years, doing street grading work. The remains will be brought to this city tomorrow and the funeral will probably be held Monday. Mrs. MacLaggan has been very sick for some time and the news of her husband's death was a severe blow to her.

The Stillwater Gazette; Front Page, May 17, 1920

DR. E. E. WELLS CALLED BEYOND AT EARLY HOUR

Nine Days With Pneumonia – Was Born at Rockford, Il., 49 years ago.

Stillwater citizens were shocked this morning when the news of the death of Dr. Ernest E. Wells, 206 South Owen street, was flashed over the city, he having been ill with pneumonia for a period of nine days. He leaves a wife and two daughters to mourn his loss. Death came in the early morning hours of Monday between 2 and 3 o'clock.

Dr. Wells had resided in Stillwater about 21 years and was well and favorably known as one of the leading physicians of the city and county. At the time of his death he held the office of county physician being appointed to that place upon his resignation as county coroner a year or so ago. At one time Dr. Wells also served as an alderman of the city of Stillwater.

Dr. Wells was born in Rockford, Illinois and at the time of his death was 49 years of age.

A sister also resides at Rockford, Ill.

He was a member of Knights Templar, Bayard Commandery of this city, Elks and other local organizations.

Funeral services will be held from his late home Wednesday afternoon at 2:30 o'clock under the auspices of the Masons of the city.

Burial will be made in Fairview Cemetery.

Eternal rest grant unto them, O Lord, and let perpetual light shine upon them. May their souls and all the souls of the faithful departed, through the mercy of God, rest in peace. Amen.

Appendix C

***Mayflower* Lineage**

John Alden was a master cooper and was hired for the *Mayflower*'s journey to America. As a master cooper, his duties consisted of making the barrels and looking after the beer and water that would be contained in them during the *Mayflower*'s journey in 1620. He married *Mayflower* passenger Priscilla Mullins around 1622 or 1623.

Mayflower Family Ancestors and Descendants

John Alden married Priscilla Mullins

Their daughter; Elizabeth Alden married William Pabodie

Their daughter; Lydia Pabodie married Daniel Grinell

Their daughter; Mary Grinell married Robert Lay III

Their son; Robert Lay IV married Jemima Pratt

Their daughter; Anna Lay married George Wright

Their son; Christopher Wright married Priscilla Cooper

Their daughter; Mary Ann Wright married William Wright

Their son; Addison Wright married Anna Maria Tobin

Their daughter; Ivy Maria Wright married John A. McLaggan

Their daughters;

Mildred M. McLaggan married Francis F. Brown

> Their children; John Frederick, Marcus Joseph, Robert Louis, Mary Evelyn, Kenneth Addison, and Florence Jane

Jeanette A. McLaggan married Merl K. Meister

> Their children; Jon Karl, Martha Jean, Michael William, Mary Wright, and Thomas

And so on . . .

Family:

*Like branches on a tree we all grow
in different directions, yet our roots remain as one*

–Unknown

ACKNOWLEDGEMENTS

would like to thank the following people who I am grateful to for their support, memories, stories, contributions, and assistance during the process of creating this ancestral and story book, which without their help would have been an even larger undertaking.

My husband, Kevin McGoldrick, for his love, support, and guidance, during this heartfelt family project.

My mother, Mary Evelyn Brown-Kirst; aunt and godmother, Florence Jane Brown-Wennerberg; first cousins-once removed, Jon Meister and Mike Meister; Aunt Mary Jean Holmberg-Brown; Uncle Kenneth Brown and Aunt Rose Brown; sons, Andrew Sherwood and Christopher Sherwood; daughter, Meghan McGoldrick; sisters, Dianne Shutt, Laurie Andreotti, Mary Jo Seidl, Susan Beck, and Frances Brabender; cousins, Julie Youngberg, Michelle Fulmer, Maribeth Wasmund, Cheryl Crosser, Colleen McKillip, and John Patrick Brown; second cousins, Becca Wilson, Susan Meister, Molly Price and Jean Juhl; second cousin once-removed, Roberta Feyereisen; nephews, Allen M. Brabender, Jake Slockbower, and Brendan McGoldrick; and first cousins once-removed, John "Mugs" McGuinness and James McGuinness.

Dave and Beth Rogers, for their genuine, welcoming attitude toward this project. I appreciate your respect for family and Stillwater history; and for the care of the former home of my great-great-grandfather, Addison Wright.

Barbara Bachmeier, Fairview Cemetery, Stillwater, Minnesota

Brent Peterson, Historian and Director of the Washington County Historical Society

Staff at St. Charles Church and St. Michael's Cemetery, Bayport, Minnesota

Staff and Volunteers at Stillwater Public Library; Minnesota Genealogical Society; and Minnesota Historical Society.

Theresa "Terri" McGoldrick

Medleybooks@gmail.com

Facebook: Theresa Lynne McGoldrick

The author and her grandsons

SELECT SOURCES

Miscellaneous records and articles collected from:

Fairview Cemetery, Stillwater, Minnesota: Burial.

Minnesota Genealogical Society, St. Paul, Minnesota: Baptismal.

Minnesota Historical Society, St. Paul, Minnesota: Newspaper articles on microfilm and digital, Probate, and Wills.

Stillwater Pubic Library, St. Croix Collection Room, Stillwater, Minnesota: Newspaper articles, and obituaries on microfilm, Kabekonian yearbooks, various books on Stillwater history.

St. Michael's Catholic Cemetery, Bayport, Minnesota: Burial.

The Library of Congress, Chronicling America: Digital Newspaper articles.

Washington County Government Center, Stillwater, Minnesota: Property and vital.

Collected from Ancestry.com

City Directories; Duluth, St. Louis, and Stillwater

Maine Marriages-1771-1907, database, Familysearch, Bangor, Penobscot, Maine

Minnesota Marriage Index, 1849-1950

Minnesota Territorial and State Censuses, Washington County, 1857, 1875

United States Federal Census, Bangor, Penobscot County, Maine, 1850

United States Federal Censuses, Duluth, St. Louis County, Minnesota, 1900, 1910

United States Federal Census, Marquette Valley, Marquette County, Wisconsin,1850

United States Federal Census, St. Joseph, St. Croix County, Wisconsin, 1870

United States Federal Censuses, Stillwater, Washington County, Minnesota 1860, 1870, 1880, 1900, 1910, 1920, 1930, 1940

U.S. National Homes for Disabled Volunteer Soldiers, 1866-1938.

Homes for Disabled Volunteer Soldiers, 1866-1938

SELECT BIBLIOGRAPHY

Alexander, Robert and Lucille. *The Wrights of Wright Street.* Durham, NY: Durham Center Museum, 1986.

Apple, Linda C. *Inspire! Writing from the Soul.* Denton, TX: AWOC.COM Publishing, 2009.

Beers, J.B., *History of Greene County, New York. With Biographical Sketches of Its Prominent Men.* NY: J.B. Beers and Co., 1884.

Day, Holly, and Sherman Wick. *Stillwater, Minnesota: A Brief History.* Charleston, SC: History Press, 2016.

Dunn, James Taylor. *The St. Croix: Midwest and Border River.* St. Paul, MN: Minnesota Historical Society Press, Reprint 1979.

Easton, Augustus B., ed. *History of the St. Croix Valley.* Chicago: H.C. Cooper, Jr. and Co., 1909.

Johnston, Patricia Condon, *Stillwater: Minnesota's Birthplace.* Afton, MN: Afton Historical Society Press, 1991.

Lammers, Rita. *Church of St. Michael, Stillwater, Minnesota 1853-2003.* Stillwater, MN: Church of St. Michael, 2002.

Larson, Agnes Mathilda. *The White Pine Industry In Minnesota: A History. Minneapoilis,* MN: University of Minnesota Press, 1949, 2007.

Martin, Albro. *James J. Hill, and The Opening of The Northwest.* St. Paul, MN: Minnesota Historical Society Press, 1991 (Original work published by Oxford University Press, NY, 1976).

Monger, George P. *Marriage Customs of the World: From Henna to Honeymoons.* Santa Barbara, CA: ABC-CLIO, 2004.

Neill, Edward, D. *The History of Washington County and the St. Croix Valley.* Minneapolis, MN: Northstar Publishing Company, 1881.

Orcutt, Wright T. *The Minnesota Lumberjack's.* Retrieved from http://collections.mnhs.org/MNHistoryMagazine/articles/6/v06i01p003-019.pdf.

Peterson, Brent T. *Stillwater: Images of America.* Charleston, SC: Arcadia Publishing, 2013.

Roney, E.L. *Looking Backward.* Roney Memorial Fund, 1970.

ENDNOTES

PART ONE
Introduction

1   Patricia Johnston Condon, *Stillwater: Minnesota's Birthplace, p. 28.*

2   Ibid, pp. 36-37.

My Mother's Request

3   Caleb Johnson, *Mayflower History*
http://mayflowerhistory.com/.

4   Henry W. Longfellow, *The Courtship of Miles Standish.* https://
www.hwlongfellow.org/poems_poem.php?pid=186

5   Ibid, https://www.hwlongfellow.org/poems_poem.php?pid=188

6   General Society of Mayflower Descendants.
www.themayflowersociety.org/

The Tobin Family

7   Bangor Maine Government. https://www.bangormaine.gov/con-
tent/2037/1495/1864/default.aspx.

8   Maine Marriages-1771–1907, database, Familysearch, Bangor, Pe-
nobsot, Maine.

9   Ibid.

10   Washington County Historical Society Timeline. Retrieved from
http://www.wchsmn.org/timeline/.

11   Admission to Minnesota into the Union 1858, https://www.sos.state.

mn.us/about-minnesota/minnesota-government/admission-of-minnesota-into-the-union-1858/

12   Agnes Larson, *When Logs and Lumber Ruled Stillwater,* p. 170.

13   James Taylor Dunn, *The St. Croix: Midwest Border River,* *p. 104.*

14   Norene Roberts, PhD, https://www.ci.stillwater.mn.us/vertical/sites/%7B5BFEF821-C140-4887-AEB5-99440411EEFD%7D/uploads/%7BE30DC583-0FB8-48D9-A66F-51F4785F39A0%7D.PDF.

15   Rita Lammers, *Church of St. Michael, Stillwater, Minnesota 1853-2003, pp. 14–15.*

16   Edward D. Neill, *The History of Washington County and the St. Croix Valley, p. 590.*

17   U.S. National Homes for Disabled Volunteer Soldiers, 1866–1938, Ancestry.com.

18   B. Peterson, (2015, October 6). *A Trip Back in Time: Burying Stillwater's Dead. Retrieved from http://www.stillwatercurrent.com/trip-back-time-burying-stillwaters-dead/.*

19   A. Brown, *Irish Railroad Workers. Retrieved from http://utahhistoricalmarkers.org/cat/rr/irish-railroad-workers.*

20   Holly Day and Sherman Wick, *Stillwater, Minnesota: A Brief History,* p. 43.

21   B. Peterson, (2015, May 5). *Lumberjack "Entertainment."* Retrieved from http://www.wchsmn.org/historical-messenger/lumberjack-en-

tertainment/.

22   James Nathan "J.N." Castle. Retrieved from https://www.leg.state.mn.us/legdb/fulldetail?ID=11600.

23   U.S. National Homes for Disabled Volunteer Soldiers, 1866–1938, Ancestry.com.

The Wright Family

24   Robert and Lucille Alexander, *The Wrights of Wright Street.*

25   *Minutes of the Wright St School 1818-1854. Transcribed by Arlene Goodwin. Retrieved from https://sites.rootsweb.com/~nygreen2/minutes_of_wright_st_school.htm.*

26   E. L. Roney, *Looking Backward*, pp. 46–47.

27   Stillwater City Directory, 1890/91, p. 43.

28   Edward D. Neill, *The History of Washington County and the St. Croix Valley, p. 581.*

29   Augustus B. Easton, *History of St. Croix Valley, Vol 1, p. 201.*

30   Patricia Johnston Condon, *Stillwater: Minnesota's Birthplace, p. 36–37*

31   E. L. Roney, *Looking Backward*, p. 63.

32   Edward D. Neill, *The History of Washington County and the St. Croix Valley, p. 608.*

Addison and Anna Maria

33   Brent Peterson, Historic Courthouse in Stillwater. Retrieved from https://patch.com/minnesota/stillwater/brent-peterson.

34   Frederick L. Beers, *History of Greene County, New York,* p. 264.

35   Lawrence E. Rogers, *History of the St. Croix, Pioneer Lawmen of The City of Stillwater, 1840–1900.*

The Bells of St. Michael's

36   Rita Lammers, *Church of St. Michael, Stillwater, Minnesota 1853-2003, pp. 37–38.*

The Joneses

37   E. L. Roney, *Looking Backward*, pp. 46–47.

The McLaggan Family

38   https://en.wikipedia.org/wiki/Whipsaw#/media/File:Pitsaw00.jpg

39   Colter (McBean), M., (1921). *Pioneer Life In New Brunswick. Transcribed by Dave Carney.*
 Retrieved from https://www.ancestry.com/mediaui-viewer/collection/1030/tree/17958471/person/1403734867/media/38f823c3-5574-4b52-8ab2-fcfc2e0bb6fa?_phsrc=IDh3562&usePUBJs=true.

PART TWO
The "Little Women" of Stillwater

40   Brent Peterson, *Stillwater: Images of America,* p. 65.

The "Little Women" of Stillwater and St. Paul

41   Stern, Alexandra Minna, PhD, Cetron, Martin, S., MD and Markel, Howard, MD PhD. *Influenza Pandemic In The United States: Lessons*

Learned and Challenges Exposed. Retrieved from https://www.ncbi.nlm.nih.gov/pmc/articles/PMC2862329/.

42   Frederick F. Brown, Retrieved from https://www.leg.state.mn.us/legdb/fulldetail?ID=11441.

43   Albro Martin, *James J. Hill, and The Opening of The Northwest, p. 580.*

44   New York Times, James J. Hill Obituary. Retrieved from http://movies2.nytimes.com/learning/general/onthisday/bday/0916.html.

45   De Luxe Theater. Retrieved from http://cinematreasures.org/theaters/31212.

46   George P. Monger, *Marriage Customs of the World" From Henna to Honeymoons, p. 98.*

47   Encephalitis Society. Retrieved from https://www.encephalitis.info/encephalitis-lethargica

48   Rita Lammers, *Church of St. Michael, Stillwater, Minnesota 1853-2003, p. 163–164.*

49   Ibid, p. 162.

50   Patricia Johnston Condon, *Stillwater: Minnesota's Birthplace*, p. 9, and back cover.

51   YMCA, Hi-Y Club. Retrieved from http://www.vintagekidstuff.com/hiy/hiy.html.

52   YWCA, Girl Reserves Club. Retrieved from http://www.vintagekidstuff.com/girlreserve/girlreserve.html.

The Adored Grandparents

53   Rita Lammers, *Church of St. Michael, Stillwater, Minnesota* 1853-2003, pp. 37 and 74.

Jean McLaggan-Meister

54   St. Michael's Catholic Church Timeline. Retrieved from https://1.
cdn.edl.io/CSf8DW71y2X45PAnoNcSbaIUH83HWQGWjgehLX4BY77p-
FGHr.pdf.

55   Rita Lammers, *Church of St. Michael, Stillwater, Minnesota 1853–
2003*, p. 118.

56   Ibid, p.119.

INDEX

Page numbers in **bold** indicate photographs.